PROTECTING
YOUR TEEN FROM
TODAY'S
WITCHCRAFT

PROTECTING
YOUR TEEN FROM
TODAY'S
WITCHCRAFT

A PARENT'S GUIDE TO CONFRONTING WICCA AND THE OCCULT

STEVE RUSSO

BETHANY HOUSE PUBLISHERS
Minneapolis, Minnesota

Published by Bethany House Publishers
11400 Hampshire Avenue South
Bloomington, Minnesota 55438

Bethany House Publishers is a division of
Baker Publishing Group, Grand Rapids, Michigan.

Printed in the United States of America

Library of Congress Cataloging-in-Publication Data

Russo, Steve, 1953-
    Protecting your teen from today's witchcraft : a parent's guide to confronting Wicca and
the occult / Steve Russo.
        p.   cm.
    Summary: "Gives parents the facts about Wicca, tips on recognizing its influence in teens,
and pracitical advice for guiding their children in the right direction"—Provided by publisher.
    ISBN 0-7642-0135-2 (pbk.)
    1. Witchcraft. 2. Occultism—Religious aspects—Christianity. 3. Teenagers—Religious
life. 4. Parenting—Religious aspects—Christianity. I. Title.

For Mom and Dad

Thanks for always believing in me,
encouraging me, and loving me.

STEVE RUSSO is the author of twelve books and numerous magazine articles. He is also the featured speaker of the music video TV show *24/SEVEN*, host of the daily radio feature *Real Answers*, and co-host of Focus on the Family's weekly teen talk radio show *Life on the Edge— Live!* Steve is a professional drummer who speaks to thousands of teens and families each year in citywide events, schools, prisons, and churches. He makes his home in Southern California.

TABLE of CONTENTS

INTRODUCTION

WELL, YOU GOT THE COURAGE to pick up this book, and now you're probably wondering what you got yourself into—let alone if you should tell your friends that you're reading a book on witchcraft.

Before we go any further, let me assure you that this book is not meant to scare or alarm you. It's designed to inform and equip you to deal with a very serious issue affecting teens today. The world of witchcraft is a difficult one to navigate through and understand. Parents want practical answers on how to deal with this issue in a sane, reasonable way. And that's why I've written this book.

Parenting has never been tougher or more confusing. And life for our kids is about the same. Every generation has its struggles. There are issues, temptations, and pain that kids must learn to handle. However, it's different for today's teens. The intensity of these struggles is greater and the pace of life is much faster than it's ever been. There's more coming at teens today than any previous generation.

Among other things, they are a generation in search of answers to the spiritual dimension of life. This search can take on many different forms and take them in many different directions—including witchcraft—as they look for power to face the difficult issues of life. About now you may be saying, "Wait a minute, my child would never get involved with witchcraft." Don't be so sure. The influence of witchcraft can be found in many places and forms—everything from comic books to prime-time television. Kids can even learn more about Wicca by taking classes on the Internet. You may also be saying, "What's so bad about Wicca? After all, isn't it about taking care of the environment and helping people to have a sense of direction and belonging? That can't be all bad." Some of the things Wicca stands for are positive. But it's the focus and methodology that we have to be concerned about.

Let's face it: Kids are curious and want to discover things for themselves. You can't force them to believe in God, or anything else, for that matter. They must come to conclusions about life and spirituality on their own. Our job as parents is not only to protect them but also to help guide them in the right direction. We need to provide them with practical resources and a safe place where they can express their thoughts and feelings. Remember, we have two ears and one mouth for a reason: We need to listen twice as much as talk—especially with teenagers!

Read this book with the intention of discussing it with your kids. And you may want to get them a copy of my companion book— *What's the Deal With Wicca?*—so they can read about it for themselves. Notice I've used the word *discuss*, not interrogate. And don't panic if you learn something that surprises you in your discussions. Be thankful that your son or daughter is running the risk of sharing their feelings with you. Be patient, understanding, and willing to take the time necessary to work through these issues together. You'll be glad you did!

One final thought. Maybe you, too, have been searching for answers to life in the spiritual dimension and have found yourself turning to witchcraft. I invite you to read this book with an open mind and examine the information provided here. There are *real* spiritual answers to the challenges of life. Look at the evidence in these pages and see if it makes sense. You've got nothing to lose and everything to gain!

CHAPTER 1:

GUESS WHO'S INTO THE CRAFT?

RIGHT NOW YOU MAY BE saying, "Wait a minute, Steve, my son or daughter would never get involved with witchcraft. After all, we go to church every Sunday, and they attend the youth group activities." Don't be so sure. Take a look at some of these stories.

I'd just finished speaking at my second high school assembly for the day, and as usual, there were a lot of students wanting to talk with me. When I talked about choices, the questions and comments from the students usually covered a variety of topics including suicide, pain, divorce, gangs, and witchcraft. This school was no different.

I noticed three students hanging back, several steps away from the rest of the crowd that was around me. Once everybody else left, they approached me.

"Thanks, Steve, for your presentation," said Emily, the short blond girl.

"Yeah," said Andrew, "we really liked what you said."

Melissa, the tall girl with short brown hair, said, "And we liked your drum playing, too. It was awesome."

"But there's one thing we want to talk with you about," said Emily. "You're not exactly right about Wicca. It's not just about power."

"Yeah," the other two added. "You're a cool guy, but we wanna help you get your facts right about Wicca."

"You gotta know this one thing, Steve," Emily went on. "We all used to be Christians, but we got turned off to being involved in church. We never found anyone there who could explain what they believed and why."

"Yeah," added Melissa, "and everyone seemed powerless, like they were already living in some kind of defeat."

"That's not how I want to spend the rest of my time on planet Earth," said Andrew.

Then, almost in unison, they said, "With Wicca we found answers and power."

They told me about all the other benefits that Wicca offers besides power, including a sense of belonging, concern for the environment, tolerance for everyone, and their beliefs—plus the ability to pick and choose what you want to believe. All three claimed to have tried Christianity but found Wicca much more appealing. Andrew said, "With Wicca you don't have to deal with hell and sin and all that other stuff they talk about in church." Melissa added, "Yeah, Steve, I just don't believe the stuff Christians teach about how you get one shot at life and then you have to go to hell. I like Wicca 'cuz of reincarnation. You can just keep trying to get it (life) right without having to worry about hell." "With Wicca, you have the freedom to believe what you want to without any restrictions," said Emily. "I can make up my own belief system that appeals to me without anyone else telling me what I have to believe."

The bell rang, and just before they headed back to class, I told them how much I appreciated their honesty and wished that we could've had more time to discuss their Wiccan beliefs. "We do, too," they responded.

Emily, Andrew, and Melissa are convinced that they found what they needed in life when they discovered Wicca.

I meet lots of teens like Emily, Andrew, and Melissa as I travel across North America. People who are sincerely trying to make sense out of life and find a way to make it work. They want a reason to get out of bed in the morning, and they want real answers to the difficult issues of life. Let's face it, there's so much stuff coming at you in the world today—families falling apart, threats of terrorism, natural disasters, unrealistic expectations from friends—and that's just the beginning of what you deal with at school, at home, and at work every day.

Many teens are looking for answers in the supernatural. They want to tap in to the source of ultimate power to change their lives—to feel special and get the relationships they want and need. Some want power to get vengeance on people who've hurt them. Pop culture's filled with allusions to witchcraft and the occult as being the source for power and all the answers to the issues of life. The fastest-growing religion today among high school and college students is Wicca. Also known as the practice of folk magick or the magick of the people, it's a contemporary pagan religion with spiritual roots in the earliest expressions of the worship of nature. For people like Emily, Melissa, and Andrew, Wicca seems to be the ticket that gave them a form of spirituality that would provide a sense of belonging, as well as some control over their own overwhelming life circumstances. The craft, as it is frequently called, also gave them the chance to create their own religion, complete with everything in spirituality that was convenient and appealed to them—including designing their own deities.

I wish I could say that I disagree with everything Melissa, Emily, and Andrew talked about, but unfortunately I can't. It's hard today to find people who attend a Christian church and can tell you why they believe in Jesus and what the Bible actually teaches. And it's true, there are a lot of people who call themselves Christians who are living defeated lives. But maybe we need to look further than just the organized Christian church for answers as to why these things happen. Because God didn't want us to be robots, He gave us the freedom of choice. This includes what we decide about Jesus and whether we decide to live by what the Bible teaches. God's power is real and it's unlimited. We must choose to either tap in to it or keep trying to do things on our own, in our own way, and with our own strength.

There are questions that keep bugging me about kids like Melissa, Emily, and Andrew. For example:

- What truths about the Christian faith have they not truly seen and known?
- Did they honestly compare the teachings of Jesus to what they learned from Wicca?

- Do they understand how unique the Bible is? Have they seen the historical, scientific, and archaeological evidence for its accuracy? Or how about the ancient manuscript support?

Sometimes the combination of life circumstances and curiosity causes us to do some exploring in the supernatural realm. Take Alexis, for example. Even though she attended church every week, she and a friend got involved with Wicca. Alexis was struggling with not having a father in her life. He'd abandoned her when she was only a year old, but it was becoming a bigger deal in her life the older she got. Alexis felt church had become routine and boring, and the youth leaders didn't seem all that concerned about the trauma she was going through. Plus, most of the kids in the youth group didn't act like they cared much about her anyway. She just didn't seem to fit in.

So Alexis and her friend checked out some books on Wicca from the library at school and became fascinated with everything they were reading. They thought it was cool so they started buying books and collecting other things related to the practice of Wicca. The two girls grew increasingly curious about whether the spells and other stuff they were reading about really worked. Alexis and her friend started experimenting and got scared by the things that were happening. Alexis became so fearful that she began carrying a knife to school, which resulted in her getting suspended. That was it—the end of the line for her. Alexis and her friend threw all the books and stuff they had been collecting in the trash. And even though she asked God to forgive her for what she'd done, Alexis still feels guilty.

A lot of kids today feel like the Christian church isn't relevant to their daily lives. One of the problems is that they've bought into a religious experience rather than establishing a personal relationship with God. It's awesome when you can grasp the concept of having an actual relationship with the living God—the God of all creation. That is one of the things that sets Christianity apart from any other religion.

Also, a lot of teens fail to really understand the resurrection power of Jesus Christ. They want answers about life and they want to be challenged to make a difference in their world—but they can't seem to find this in their churches. Some teens even question if God really cares about them and what's going on in their life. They want to know where God was when their mother died of cancer or why their father lost his job and abandoned the family. One girl asked me where God was when she was gang-raped. Disappointment with God is real for a lot of kids today. Obviously, pain and suffering are part of life—but it's still hard to handle. And in some situations, we may never know the reason why we experience some of the things that we do in life.

In other situations, leaders in the church have failed miserably at making the Christian faith clear and understandable to kids in need of answers for the problems they're dealing with. The lack of practically applying the Bible to everyday life has caused many kids to search elsewhere, including witchcraft, for help and hope. Unfortunately, some leaders and Bible teachers seem to be answering all the questions that no one's asking.

Wicca's got a very positive image in our society today. It's no longer some ridiculed set of beliefs based on superstition. Instead, it's become a mainstream religious system that many see as a valid alternative to an "outdated Christian faith." There are at least five major ways in which Wicca differs from Christianity and other religions:

- worship of the goddess and god;
- reverence for the earth;
- acceptance of magick;
- acceptance of reincarnation;
- lack of proselytizing activities (trying to get someone to change their religious beliefs).[1]

Wicca (or witchcraft) is popping up everywhere. You can find its influence in PC games, movies, music, prime-time TV shows, cartoons, and books. The number of Web sites on Wicca is growing, and there are even classes being offered online and in some public libraries. So why is Wicca so popular, especially with teens?

For many, Wicca's promise of personal power over others and the ability to control your own life seems irresistible—even among some teens currently involved in the church. Wicca is admired for its sensitivity to the environment and is seen as the female-friendly religion in comparison to Christianity's supposedly male-dominated hierarchical

---

[1]Scott Cunningham, *The Truth About Witchcraft Today* (St. Paul, MN: Llewellyn Publications, 1997), 62.

system. And because Christianity is perceived as being judgmental and intolerant in today's society, it's easy to see Wicca's huge appeal. Wiccans feel like they belong without the baggage of having to look, walk, or talk a certain way. Plus, because Wicca rejects moral absolutes, a person's natural rebellious nature is appealed to. And it offers the chance to develop a personal self-styled religion. The bottom line is that Wicca offers its followers the ability to set things right on their own without having to rely on a God who doesn't seem to answer their prayers anyway.

So who's right? Emily, Andrew, and Melissa? Did Alexis and her friend somehow miss the point of Wicca and quit too soon? Does Christianity really offer the answers and power we need and want? How do we make sense out of life?

Wicca and Christianity both can't be right. Ultimately, you and your teen will have to decide which pathway is the right one for you to pursue. But remember to choose wisely and make sure that you honestly compare what Jesus teaches and what Wicca teaches. It's not good enough to just be sincere in your beliefs. Sincerity won't get you very far when it comes to your eternal destiny or making life work on planet Earth. Neither will it give you the power for living in a stress-filled, confusing world. Maybe you know others who are into Wicca and you're trying to understand and help them. This book will help you to discover the truth about Wicca and its exploding popularity.

Examine the information in this book carefully. Don't be afraid to ask yourself and your teen the tough questions. Think about it logically. In the end, I hope that you'll discover the answers you're looking for to make sense out of this issue, as well as life and eternity.

CHAPTER 2:

WHAT'S THE WORLD OF A TEENAGER REALLY LIKE?

DO YOU REMEMBER YOUR teenage years? For some it's a longer trip down memory lane than for others! What was contemporary culture like? What were your major concerns in life?

I spend considerable time on public school campuses each year in North America and overseas. I do an assembly program for middle school, junior high, and high school kids on how to make better choices. My presentation begins with a drum solo to get the kids' attention, and most of the time after the assembly I have a few minutes to talk with kids individually. You would not believe what I see and hear on these campuses.

In addition to the face-to-face encounters I have with teens, I also spend two hours on Saturday nights co-hosting a radio show produced by Focus on the Family. It's a live call-in show for teens called *Life on the Edge—Live!* My co-host, Susie Shellenberger, and I hear it all—from witchcraft to body mod to self-mutilation to parents who are in jail to kids struggling with alternative lifestyles. I often say to kids who call in, "I wish I had an island somewhere that I could invite you to visit, where you could rest, heal, and be encouraged."

Things are definitely a lot different than when you and I were teenagers.

That's why it's so important for parents and those who work with teens to do everything they can to gain a better understanding of this generation. The Bible puts it this way:

> From the tribe of Issachar, there were 200 leaders of the tribe with their relatives. All these men understood the temper of the times and knew the best course for Israel to take. (1 Chronicles 12:32)

Because these leaders understood the "signs of the times," their knowledge and judgment was helpful in making decisions for the nation. It's equally important for parents to know what is happening in the world of their teen in order to best plan a course of action for helping them navigate through the issues of life. Knowledge of current events, trends, and needs can help you better understand your teen's thoughts and attitudes. This information can also help you guide them in using God's Word in a relevant way to make decisions for their situation.

So what is the world of a teenager really like today?

CONTEMPORARY CULTURE

Think about the contemporary culture in which teens live. Howard Stern exemplifies our culture's growing tolerance for grossness. What about the NBA's "basketbrawl" involving Indiana's Ron Artest and Detroit Pistons' fans? Think about Nicole Richie and Paris Hilton on *The Simple Life*, or the latest reality TV shows. And we don't want to leave out Janet Jackson and Justin Timberlake's Super Bowl fiasco or a former president's definition of what sex is. And don't think surfing the Web, reading blogs, entering chat rooms, and typing IMs is innocent either.

Now imagine being with me on a junior high campus and noticing two armed guards standing on either side of me during my assembly program. Or maybe you're with me on a high school campus in a very upscale neighborhood, where kids attend whose parents have very prestigious jobs with the government. After the assembly we stay to talk with kids during lunch. As soon as the bell rings, huge cyclone fences drop out of the ceiling to cage kids in during the lunch period to keep them from leaving school, to curb potential violence, and to stop unwanted visitors from coming on campus. Metal detectors are becoming more commonplace in schools. But even metal detectors couldn't stop the tragedy that happened on a high school campus in Red Lake, Minnesota. It's almost surreal that student Jeffrey Weise would fatally shoot seven people at school, then kill himself. It was like the Columbine tragedy all over again.

Life is a minefield of potentially explosive issues and experiences: drugs, alcohol, violence, gangs, and bullying. Suicide is one of the leading killers of teens in America today. Every teen I have ever talked with who has attempted to kill him or herself has told me the same thing: "Steve, I really didn't want to die, I just wanted the pain to stop."

Teens today live in a society where sex sells everything from vitamins to cars to burgers. And it's taking a toll on our kids. A teen girl who called *Life on the Edge—Live!* was bothered by a male friend whom she had turned to for encouragement during a tough time at home, who played along with her and then wanted "benefits"—sex. I've lost track of the number of teen guys who have called the show or e-mailed us because they are struggling with Internet porn.

Young adults who as teenagers took pledges not to have sex until marriage were just as likely to contract a venereal disease as people who didn't make the promise, according to a study in the Journal of Adolescent Health. After examining the data from this government-funded study, sociologists concluded that there was no statistically significant difference between the percentage of people who took the virginity pledge and were infected with an STD, and those who didn't pledge.[1]

The study found that 88 percent of sexually active people who took the abstinence pledge had intercourse before marriage. It also revealed that teens who took the pledge were less likely to get tested and treated for venereal disease.

But it's not just cyberspace sex that teens are struggling with—it's real-life stuff as well. Take for example "friends with benefits"—casual sexual relationships. For those who pursue these relationships, they typically involve oral sex (78 percent) and/or sexual intercourse (79 per-

---

[1]"Sex Vows Did Not Curb STDs," *Los Angeles Times*, March 20, 2005, A20.

cent).[2] NBC News and *People* magazine commissioned a landmark national poll on teen sex. Here are some of the results[3]:

- Nearly three in ten (27 percent) thirteen- to sixteen-year-olds are sexually active and "have been with someone in an intimate way."[4]
- Sexual activity is much more common among fifteen- to sixteen-year-olds (41 percent) than thirteen- to fourteen-year-olds (14 percent).
- Engaging in oral sex is more common among fifteen- to sixteen-year-olds (19 percent) than thirteen- to fourteen-year-olds (4 percent).
- Young teens are as likely to have had sexual intercourse as oral sex. But their reasons for doing so are somewhat different. Among the 13 percent of young teens who have had sexual intercourse, more than half say a principal reason they did so for the first time was because they met the right person (62 percent). This is consistent with the majority's view that it is very important to be in love before having intercourse (68 percent).
- While nearly all young teens (90 percent) know they can get an STD from having sexual intercourse, they're not always acting on that knowledge. Only two in three (67 percent) say they use protection such as condoms every time they have sex.

A 2004 Columbia University study found that while many participants in abstinence programs delay sex for eighteen months, 88 percent still had sex before marriage and had STD rates similar to others their age.[5]

POP CULTURE

We will talk more about pop culture in the media in a later chapter, but just think about the themes of TV shows, movies, bestselling book series, and even comics. Witchcraft and the occult are everywhere.

---

[2]*MSNBC.com*, January 27, 2005.

[3]Ibid.

[4]*MSNBC.com*, January 27, 2005.

[5]"Special Report: Young Teens & Sex," *People* magazine, January 31, 2005, 95.

Have you looked at a comic book lately? Have you noticed how dark they've become?

Or how about video games? A key sequence in *Grand Theft Auto: San Andreas* requires a player to steal a police or SWAT team tank, machine-gun rival gang members, and incinerate employees of a rival crack dealer—acts all covered by the Adults Only rating—increased from its original Mature rating—prominently displayed on each copy of the video game.

That rating, however, hasn't stopped countless underage players from picking up virtual Uzis in the latest GTA installment, the top-selling game of 2004. Advocacy groups say exposure to such material makes kids more aggressive and desensitizes them to real-world violence, an argument that's winning increasing support from state and local lawmakers looking to ban the sale of such games to minors.[6]

MUSIC

Music is one of the most powerful, and underestimated, influences in the life of a teenager. It's like a private language for every generation. Music has the power to alter our opinions, attitudes, values, beliefs, relationships, and lifestyle choices.[7] But for a lot of teens, they don't recognize how powerful this influence is in their lives. It becomes a dangerous blind spot. Everywhere they go and in just about everything they do, they are surrounded by music. Teens spend an average of four to six hours per day interacting with mass media of different forms.

Not only do we listen to it on iPods, MP3 players, computers, and in our cars, but it's also in the stores where we shop, in the restaurants where we eat, and in the movies that we watch. Can you imagine how dull an adventure film would be without the musical background to add excitement? Where would the heroes be without their theme songs? What about an extreme-sports show without music? We live in a music-saturated culture.

Studies have revealed that the average teen listens to more than ten thousand hours of music between the seventh and twelfth grades—and that doesn't include watching thousands of hours of MTV. Anything we are exposed to this much has got to have an influence on us.

[6]David Becker, "When Games Get Gory," *CNET News.com*, February 22, 2005.
[7]George Barna, *Real Teens* (Ventura, CA: Regal Books, 2001), 73.

Eighteen-year-old Todd says that music is the most important thing in his life: "The CDs, concerts, lights, the whole atmosphere—it's my salvation. If things bother me, I'll go into my room and lock the door, turn on the stereo, and escape into my own world. I can just space. Music is a lot cheaper than drugs, and it's legal. Sometimes I'll smoke a little pot and space for a couple of hours, which is cool—but I don't need the pot. I'm a music freak! It's the place I'm the happiest. So why not indulge my music habit, even though it takes most of my cash? It's better than a drug habit or some other form of meaningless entertainment."

Teens identify with music, and it helps them express their feelings, problems, joys, and beliefs. Music reflects and directs the teen culture. Music often tells the story of our times, highlighting the struggles and issues facing our society, like abortion, racial tension, violence, and AIDS. Take, for example, a concert that was scheduled to take place in St. Petersburg, Florida, by a hard-rock band called Hell on Earth. The group had planned to feature an onstage suicide of a terminally ill person during their concert to raise awareness of right-to-die issues. The band is known for outrageous onstage stunts like chocolate-syrup wrestling and grinding up live rats in a blender.

Band leader Billy Tourtelot sent an e-mail out to fans the week before the concert and said, "This show is far more than a typical Hell on Earth performance. This is about standing up for what you believe in, and I am a strong supporter of physician-assisted suicide." In response to the band's plan, the city council approved an emergency ordinance making it illegal to conduct a suicide for commercial or entertainment purposes, and to host, promote, and sell tickets for such an event. The owner of the Palace Theater in downtown St. Petersburg then canceled the concert.

Now, I'm all for speaking out on issues in our culture, but I also think there are appropriate ways to address each problem. In this situation, Hell on Earth should have found a better way to express their feelings.

For millions of teens, music produces a lifestyle to adopt and cultural heroes to look up to and imitate. Music directs what teens do by influencing the way they style their hair, the clothes they wear, and even the kind of language they use. Singers, songwriters, and bands often set the pace for a variety of trends that influence the way teens (and adults) think and what they do. In a way, you could say that musicians are teachers trying to communicate a message to teens about how they should live. And a lot of teens I meet have been listening to these messages.

SCHOOL

Public education has changed dramatically in the last twenty years. There used to be the three Rs, now we have four: reading, 'riting, 'rithmetic, and reproductive rights. Our schools have become battlefields for a wide array of causes and issues—school-based clinics, values clarification, evolution, self-esteem, tolerance, and gay awareness. The dropout rate is increasing, and we are just waking up to the long-term effects of the literacy problem. Kids are being alienated from their parents, and traditional morality has been traded for relativism. Kids are being taught to rationalize rather than discern. We've certainly come a long way from the days of the little red schoolhouse.

Schools have shifted the emphasis from cognitive skills (facts, information) to affective skills (feelings, attitudes). Some dubbed this as "therapy education" and a new jargon was designed to promote it. These terms include behavior modification, values clarification, higher critical thinking, holistic education, and moral reasoning.

So how is the culture affecting teens—in their thinking, feelings, and attitudes?

Teens today are more complex, confusing, mobile, info-drenched, and self-sufficient than previous generations. In order to better interact with them, we need to understand what they're thinking, how they're feeling, and what motivates them. They possess tremendous energy, potential, and a dedication to make a difference in the world around them.

So let's start with some foundational things. Researcher George Barna has called the newest generation, those born between 1984–2002, "the Mosaics."[8] This term communicates a lot about this generation. Teens are mosaic because

---

[8]Ibid., 12.

- their lifestyles are an eclectic combination of traditional and alternative activities;
- they are the first generation of Americans among whom the majority will exhibit a nonlinear style of thinking—a mosaic, connect-the-dots-however-you-choose approach;
- their relationships are much more racially integrated and fluid than any we have seen in U.S. history;
- their core values are the result of a cut-and-paste mosaic of feelings, facts, principles, experiences, and lessons;
- their primary information and connection—the Internet—is the most bizarre, inclusive, and ever-changing pastiche of information ever relied upon by humankind;
- the central spiritual tenets that provide substance to their faith are a customized blend of multiple-faith views and religious practices.[9]

Young people think differently than adults do; they don't always think logically. For example, when I've talked with some teens involved in Wicca about power and how they can obtain it, they haven't totally thought it through. One girl said, "Steve, when I need power, I pick up a rock or crystal and channel all my power into it. Then I wait for the rock or crystal to give me the power back again." My response was, "If you have to give this rock or crystal power, so you can get it back, then you don't end up with any more power than you started with." That's when her blank stare told me she had not "connected all the dots" yet.

Teens have grown up in a postmodern, relativistic world where there's no absolute truth and all striving is said to be worthless and in vain since there's no meaning to be gained. Seven out of ten teens say there is no absolute moral truth, and eight out of ten teens claim that truth is relative to the individual and his or her circumstances.[10]

While family, friendships, and personal achievement are important, experiences are what rule teens' lives. The constant that keeps life meaningful and invigorating is the latest and most satisfying experience.[11]

The one word that seems to be in the frontal lobes of most teens'

[9]Ibid., 17.
[10]Ibid., 92.
[11]Ibid., 43.

philosophy of life is *whatever*. Combine their world views, values, and mosaic style of thinking, and you will realize that they're incredibly comfortable with a number of contradictions in their lives. As parents, it's vitally important that we are at least aware of the existence of these contradictions and can recognize them in our teens' lives. But keep in mind, they are most likely unable to explain why they feel the way they do. Here are a few examples:

- Teens are optimistic about the future, despite feeling unfulfilled in the present.
- Most teenagers feel driven to achieve success, although they are confused about meaning, purpose, and direction in life.
- Most teens are highly interested in spirituality, but comparatively few are engaged in the pursuit of spiritual depth.
- Millions of teenagers have been deeply wounded by their family, yet most of them have a deep commitment to achieving family health in the future.
- Teenagers are renowned for their relational emphasis, yet their pool of closest friends changes regularly.
- Six out of ten teenagers believe that the Bible is accurate; at the same time, even larger numbers of teens reject many of the Bible's core teachings.
- The parents of teenagers have the greatest level of influence upon the faith of teens, in spite of teens and their parents spending little time interacting with regard to spirituality.
- Most teens acknowledge that gaining understanding into moral truth is critical, but relatively few take the time to arrive at a workable conclusion to the matter.[12]

For many in this generation, Wicca seems to offer an ideal spiritual fit. Teens are perfectly comfortable with the experiential-based, build-your-own-belief-system, relative-truth approach to religion. It allows for mosaic-style thinking and tolerance.

CHALLENGES THAT CONCERN THEM THE MOST

Being a teenager isn't easy these days. There's an overabundance of information, challenges, opportunities, pressures, and choices that they

---

[12]Ibid., 60–63.

must meet head on. Stress levels begin to rise as they think about the challenges they face. But amazingly, their list of concerns is relatively small—less than a dozen.

The number-one issue for teens these days relates to educational achievement. Four out of every ten teenagers named the challenges related to education as their top focus. They pursue educational achievement because they recognize it as a gateway to independence, self-definition, and material success.

The rest of the list includes (in order):

1. Financial needs related to current family hardships.
2. The stress and pressure of juggling multiple tasks and performing well.
3. Problems with friends, relational difficulties with parents and family members.
4. Substance abuse, time pressures, and restraints.
5. Career concerns, physical threats.
6. Personal financial problems.
7. Health issues.[13]

Okay, so how's a parent supposed to connect all these dots?

How do you make sense of it all? Stop trying to think logically and totally rationally when it comes to your teenager. You won't be able to predict their behavior, because what you see isn't always what you get.

Start looking at the big picture, and in the process work at breaking down relational barriers that may exist. Work at listening carefully to the fundamental basis of their dreams, ideas, and the way they react to opportunities. Don't nitpick at their views or tell them how inane their ideas are. Instead, dialogue with them and help them to think more deeply about their dreams and opportunities. Take a more Socratic approach. The philosopher Socrates reasoned with his students and taught by asking questions. Our objective as parents should be to get our teens to think, not just feel and put all the bits and pieces they've embraced from our culture together.

Bridging the emotional gap starts by parents unconditionally accepting their teen for what they believe and who they are. It means invading their world by earning the right to be heard, spending more time in meaningful dialogue, and affirming your love for them.

---

[13]Ibid., 80–81.

CHAPTER 3:

DABBLING IN THE DARKNESS

AS A CHILD I DISTINCTLY remember my mom and dad consistently warning me not to play with matches or fire. There were two consequences that they always emphasized. First, I could get burned. Second, I could burn the house down. But no matter how much my parents told me not to play with matches or fire, there seemed to be this uncontrollable desire I had inside to dabble with it. It was a subtle seduction of sorts.

When I was nine or ten years old, my brother and I decided to experiment with fire in the basement of our big old house in northern California. We gathered several candles from the house, found some old bottles to put them in, and ran down to the basement. We carefully set the candles in various places in the basement, even up in the narrow crawl space right underneath the floor of the house. Then the fun began; we lit each candle and turned out the lights. It was a bit scary at first with the lights turned out, but was it ever cool-looking—that is, until Mom came down the steps and saw what we had done. I don't recall all the words she used to communicate her anxiety except, "Do you realize that you could have burned down the house? Just wait till your father gets home and sees what you two have done." Needless to say, Dad was not a happy camper when he found out we'd been playing with fire!

Teens today are being subtly deceived and seduced by the devil to dabble with fire, too—spiritual fire. They aren't saying much about Satan's seduction in their lives because most of them don't know that he's at the heart of it. He's a great deceiver. He doesn't march into their lives accompanied by a loud brass band. He slyly worms his way in through the opportunities they and we give him. And since many teens haven't been taught what the Bible says about Satan's strategies, they often blame themselves, and their confusion, fear, and sense of guilt further contributes to their silence.

What are parents, Sunday school teachers, youth workers, and pastors to do in the face of this assault? Let's begin by stating what we can't do.

First, we can't bury our heads in the sand. This is not the time to respond in denial or claim that our Christian kids are immune to this kind of problem. Satan's seductive activities are aimed at destroying the church at its point of greatest vulnerability: the family. The enemy is after Christian families in general and the families of Christian leaders in particular.

Second, we can't run in fear. Remember: Satan is a defeated foe who's running out of time—he'll be ultimately vanquished when Jesus returns. The war against the spiritual seduction of our teens is a winnable one. If we retreat instead of advance, we forfeit ground to the enemy that doesn't belong to him. We must exert our authority in Jesus Christ and claim His victory in the lives of our teens.

That's why we need to become more aware of the spiritual nature of the world we live in. Our teens are growing up in a seductive, relative-truth culture. Many of the things that surround them are subtly influenced by the occult or witchcraft. The occult is a set of mostly unrelated divination and/or spiritual practices or activities that appear to tap into forces that have not been explained by science, and which are not conventional practices seen in traditional religions.

Parents must grasp how parenting styles can either assist or block the resolution of a teen's spiritual conflicts. Later in the book we will address the topics of parental identity, styles of parenting, and parenting skills.

Ultimately, this spiritual battle is going to be won or lost "between our ears." In essence, it's a battle for our minds and emotions. That's why it's so important to help our teens guard themselves from activities that are entryways into the world of the occult.

DOORWAYS TO THE DARK

What warped thoughts is Satan sneaking into your teen's mind? Let's take a look at a national study of teenagers.[1] The research was designed and conducted by the Barna Research Group, Ltd.

PSYCHIC AND SUPERNATURAL ACTIVITIES	PERCENTAGE WHO HAVE TRIED IT:
• Read or looked at your horoscope	79%
• Used a Ouija board	35%
• Read a book about witchcraft or Wicca	34%
• Had your palm read	30%
• Played a game that featured witchcraft or psychic elements	28%
• Had your fortune told	27%
• Been physically present when someone was using their psychic or supernatural powers	14%
• Participated in a séance	10%
• Visited a medium or some other spiritual guide, not including a pastor, priest, or rabbi	9%
• Called or seen a psychic	9%
• Tried to cast a spell or mix a magical potion	8%

What do you think so far? Is Satan influencing the thinking of teenagers?

---

[1]George Barna, *Teens and the Supernatural* (Ventura, CA: WisdomWorks Ministries, May 2002).

You should be convinced that if your teen dabbles in these activities, they are opening a doorway to the darkness they will later regret.

PLAYING WITH FIRE

The following games and activities entice and encourage teens to experiment with the supernatural. They are closely linked with Satanism and the occult. Just what are the problems with the occult activities? The explanations should help you understand why you and your teens should stay away from any involvement with these activities.

Astral projection describes an out-of-body travel experience. Astral is a realm of existence parallel to physical reality but slightly apart from it. In this realm, the nonmaterial body may pass through both time and space. A wide variety of entities inhabit the astral: elementals (gnomes, salamanders, fairies, leprechauns, tree maidens, dragons, elves, dwarfs, trolls, goblins), and the conscious or dreaming presence of living individuals (ghosts).

Occultists define it as the conscious separation of the astral body from the physical body, resulting in an altered state of consciousness and sometimes in different qualities of perception. In reality, astral projection is nothing more than a mind trip.

Your teen needs to know that Christians should not seek astral projection experiences. We will separate from our bodies only once for the purpose of being with the Lord (2 Corinthians 5:6–8). Anything else is a demonic counterfeit.

Table lifting has many variations. It's usually played as a party game in which kids try to lift an object with powers other than physical strength. Even though it is not intended to conjure up something evil, bad things often result because such activities are concerted efforts to tap into the supernatural.

Warn your teen that deliberately trying to call upon supernatural powers apart from God is never good. It's the same thing Satan tempted Christ to do when he asked Him to use His supernatural powers independent of God the Father (Matthew 4:1–11). If the "game" works, you can be sure that the power that appears is not God's.

Fortune-telling is an attempt to predict the future through divination, which is the magickal art of discovering the unknown by interpreting random patterns or symbols. Tools such as clouds, tarot cards, flames, or smoke are used. Divination contacts the psychic mind by tricking or drowsing the conscious mind through ritual and by observing or manipulating tools. All occultic practices claim to enable people to know the future or be able to read minds. The lure of knowledge and power is a powerful hook for the naïve, and our teens are especially vulnerable to it.

Satan doesn't have perfect knowledge of the future, nor does he know what a believer is thinking. But he does know more than can be humanly explained. Alert your teen that we are not to consult mediums or spiritists (Leviticus 19:31; 20:6; 20:27). A medium is a person that has the ability to become a middle ground between our world and the world of the dead, therefore allowing the dead to speak through him or her. We are to trust God for tomorrow and live responsible lives today.

Astrology is a system based on the belief that celestial bodies influence human beings. Astrologers claim that an individual is affected by the cosmic array that existed in the heavens at the time of his birth. Each person was born under the influence of one of the twelve signs of the zodiac. Astrologers plot the heavens and read the "signs" (horoscope) for the purposes of gaining insight into a person's character and personality. Mundane astrology deals with large-scale phenomena (e.g., wars, natural disasters, political trends, and the destiny of nations). Horary astrology determines the implications of undertaking particular actions at certain times. Horary is a branch of astrology dealing with questions regarding any important matter. A chart is created for the time when the person's mind is most strongly focused on the matter in question.

More people read their horoscope each day than read the Bible. Some say they read their horoscopes only for fun; they don't really believe them. That shows a pathetic misunderstanding of how the mind works. Suppose your teen reads in her horoscope that she should beware of strangers today. She may laugh about it, but when she meets a stranger later in the day, guess what thought is still fresh in her mind? The fact that she didn't believe her horoscope didn't stop the power of suggestion from planting the idea in her mind. Educate your teen that astrology is a counterfeit guidance system based on nothing more than chance. It should be avoided.

Crystals or pyramids. Crystals are mystical symbols of the spirit because they are solid and tangible while also being transparent. Among many shaman groups, natural crystals are power objects. The word *pyramid* means "glorious light," from the Greek word *pyros* for fire. Crystals and pyramids are routinely associated with the New Age movement (the growing penetration of Eastern and occultic mysticism into Western culture) and the occult. If your teen is playing around with crystals or pyramids, she is probably involved with other New Age or occultic practices.

Spirit guides are nothing more than demonic voices. Occultic conferences have meditative practices that enable people to acquire their own spirit guides. Some spirits come by the laying on of hands, others through guided imagery or a mediumistic trance.

Ouija board. A sixth-grade teacher in Southern California made the headlines of his local newspaper when he refused to remove a Ouija board from his classroom. He saw nothing wrong with the game and felt his First Amendment rights were at stake. Concerned parents went to the school board calling for the game's removal.

The Ouija board (the name is simply a combination of the French and German words for *yes*) has been around in various forms since the sixth century B.C. The modern Parker Brothers game board has the numbers zero through nine, the alphabet, and the words *good, bye, yes,* and *no* printed on the surface. A teardrop-shaped pointer is placed on the board.

Two players face each other over the board with their fingers lightly resting on the pointer, with the intention of allowing it to move freely. The players ask guidance questions relating to such things as career, relationships, investments, gambling, and health, and wait for the counter to spell out the answers. The game has allegedly been used for contacting the dead and the living, contacting the spirit realm, developing psychic powers, and finding lost belongings.

How or why the game works is a mystery—even to the manufacturer. The instructions include the statement, "If you use it in a frivolous spirit, asking ridiculous questions, laughing over it, you naturally get undeveloped influences around you."[2] What are these "undeveloped influences"? Some of what happens on the board is from the subconscious mind of the operator, but some information reflects contact with demons, and the game has been linked to a variety of spiritual conflicts. Satanists have been known to crash Ouija board parties to help players learn how to really use the game.

The Ouija board is clearly a form of divination, which is repeatedly forbidden in the Bible.

I Ching or *Book of Changes*. This is an ancient Chinese volume of collective wisdom. It is consulted in conjunction with casting yarrow sticks or tossing coins. Patterns formed by the sticks or coins are said to reveal subconscious tendencies that the I Ching glyphs and hexagrams interpret spiritually and psychologically.

Automatic writing is practiced by spiritual mediums. The medium enters a trance and writes down the impressions that come to mind. It is an obvious counterfeit of the prophetic voice of God. God works through the active minds of His people, but occultic practices require a passive state of the mind. The occult actually bypasses the mind and the personality of the person involved, and a different personality emerges. Your children should be warned to leave any gathering where automatic writing or other mediumistic practices are taking place.

Tarot is a system of symbolic images. The cards are ancestors of modern playing cards and were originally designed as tools for divination. A set of seventy-eight cards, which carry pictures and symbols, are used to connect the user with the collective unconscious in order to get information about a person or situation. The cards can be used to determine the past, present, and future of an event or person and can become powerful tools in magickal workings and rituals. No one really knows the specific origin of the cards. Christians should not have anything to do with tarot cards or any other type of divination (Deuteronomy 18:10–11).

Palm reading or *palmistry* is the study and interpretation of the palm of the hand for the purpose of divination. Distinguishing features of the palm include whorls and line patterns and the color and texture of the skin. People have their palms read because they want insight into themselves or the future.

---

[2] *www.museumoftalkingboards.com/directio.html.*

God speaks to such acts of divination:

> But the angel of the Lord told Elijah ... "Go and meet the messengers of the king of Samaria and ask them, 'Why are you going to Baal-zebub, the god of Ekron, to ask whether the king will get well? Is there no God in Israel?'" (2 Kings 1:3).

> So why are you trying to find out the future by consulting mediums and psychics? Do not listen to their whisperings and mutterings. Can the living find out the future from the dead? Why not ask your God? "Check their predictions against my testimony," says the LORD. "If their predictions are different from mine, it is because there is no light or truth in them" (Isaiah 8:19–20).

Your teens must learn to ask God to search their hearts and trust Him for their future instead of turning to established practices of divination such as palm reading.

Bloody Mary. There are a couple of different versions of this game that are played in a dark bathroom and are an invitation to demonic powers.

In one version it is said that the player chants, "Bloody Mary, bloody Mary," until invisible claws scratch his face and draw blood. In another version, a pseudo out-of-body experience, based on the classic horror movie *Poltergeist* occurs. After chanting "Bloody Mary" in the dark bathroom, the player allows his mind to enter the mirror and travel to a particular destination—a friend's house, a store, etc. It's amazing how many kids see this game as a cute trick, not realizing that this casual clash with the occult is a dangerous first step into the world of spiritism.

Blood pacts. There isn't a more obvious counterfeit to Christianity than making a blood pact. We are united with Christ and with each other through the sacrifice of Jesus Christ. His shed blood is the basis for Christian birthright and fellowship. Any other blood pact is a valueless perversion of Christ's work.

Satanists commonly draw blood and drink it at their ceremonies. It is a counterfeit of Christian communion, in which we eat the flesh and drink the blood of Christ by faith. Blood pacts have taken on a romantic notion among kids who become blood brothers and sisters by pricking their fingers and mingling their blood. Whether it is a childish game or a serious ritual, it must be renounced.

We have only scratched the surface in exploring games and activities with occultic orientation, and I have no idea what kinds of harmful games will be introduced in the future. Guard your teen against an apparent recreational diversion that in reality may be a first step into the enemy's domain.

NOTORIOUS GAMES

For as long as there've been PC games, there's been concern about what possible effects they may have on the minds and emotions of kids. The gaming industry has become the fastest-growing sector in the entertainment business to the tune of $24 billion per year. According to a recent survey by Nielsen Media Research, thirteen- to seventeen-year-old gamers now spend an average of $30 a month on video and computer games.[3]

Sometimes parents have trouble understanding not only the appeal of these games but also how to play them. You could say it's a classic "generation gap" situation. Parents were raised on passive media—TV, newspapers, radio, and billboards. They can generally only cope with 1.7 channels of communication at once. Teens have been raised on media that is frenetic, multisensory, and interactive. They can simultaneously master 5.4 channels of communication including surfing the Internet, text messaging, and talking on the phone.

So what kinds of themes and content do these games contain? *PC Gamer* magazine came up with what they have called "The 10 Most Controversial Games of All Time."[4]

10. *Shadow Warrior*: The game is a first-person shooter that follows the adventures of crouching ninja Lo Wang. Japanese-Americans were feeling like their cultural heritage had been reduced to offensive clichés. The game didn't make much of a lasting impression, so it came and went—along with the controversy.

9. *Carmageddon*: A 3D game that puts you in a lethal car race,

---

[3]Richard Verrier, "At 50, Disneyland Boots Up Its Quest for the Fountain of Youth," Sunday, May 1, 2005, A28.
[4]*PC Gamer,* May 2003, Volume 10, Number 5, 50–51.

and you earn money by causing damage that includes running over ill-fated pedestrians. The big concern was the glorification of ramming innocent bystanders into cars, making them bloody hood ornaments—all for money. Amazingly, the original Carmageddon ended up being ported to a bunch of consoles, including the more kiddy-oriented Game Boy Color. (*Porting* is when a computer game is designed to run on one platform—personal computer or video game console—but converted to run on a different platform.)

8. *Duke Nukem 3D*: The main character of this first-person 3D shooter game, Duke, is an over-muscular psycho who defends the earth from aliens. The storm over this game was Duke's forking out dollar bills to strippers who shed their clothes, or putting suffering (and nude) women who would plead with him, "Killll meeee," out of their misery. In spite of the game's sexism, a sequel is being developed.

7. *Phantasmagoria*: The main character in this game is a young wife exposing the secrets of a deadly old mansion that she just moved into. The controversy this game has caused comes as a result of blood and gore, sex, partial nudity, and a brutal rape scene. Even though the game had a self-censoring option, Australia banned it completely, and some stores in the U.S. refused to sell it. In spite of the controversy, a sequel was spawned.

6. *Soldier of Fortune*: The main character is John Mullins, a mercenary-for-hire. The object of the game is to find four stolen nukes, dispatching any assorted scum who interfere. The charge here: The action was a little too realistic. *SOF*'s location-sensitive damage model lets you blow off body parts, leaving bloody stumps and howls of pain from those injured. The all-too-human enemies begged for their lives and doubled over in agony after searing shots to the groin. It still seems to hold the title of "goriest video game" of all time.

5. *Kingpin*: The player is the shooter who assumes the identity of a two-bit thug who whacks targets with lead pipes, flamethrowers, grenades, and shotguns. This game's abundant blood and smack-talking obscenities put it in the hot seat of controversy. Inevitably, the game tried way too hard to be notorious—the four-letter language and the cartoonish violence outdid each other—and the developer, Xatrix, went out of business soon after the game's release.

4. *Everquest*: This fantasy-based MMORPG (massively multi-player online role-playing game; RPG means role-playing game) subtly draws players into a persistent online world where they could live virtually forever—as long as they keep paying their monthly subscription fees. Dozens, hundreds, and even thousands of people can play a game all at the same time. Everquest showed up on the controversy map after the highly publicized Thanksgiving 2001 suicide of Shawn Woolley. His mother alleges that Shawn killed himself because he was addicted to EQ. The game is as popular as ever and continues to experience phenomenal growth, despite Mrs. Woolley's threatened lawsuit to require warning labels advising that EQ is dangerously addictive.

3. *Panty Raider*: An "adventure game" where the player is supposed to help sex-crazed aliens take pictures of scantily clad models. If the player doesn't help the aliens, they will destroy the world. Because of Raider's immature sex antics, it was taunted to CNN and *USA Today* as an example of videogaming's degradation of women. Unfortunately, all the controversy actually helped sell more copies of the game than it would have without all the free publicity.

2. *Postal*: In this action game, the player is an armed loony who goes on a major killing spree. The problem with Postal is that the goal is not to gun down criminals, demons, or aliens—the targets are the innocent human citizens living in a small town. Naturally, those who work for the U.S. Postal Service were offended by the game. In spite of the controversy, Postal 2 is in the works and promises to be even more twisted than the original.

1. *Doom*: This is the game that revolutionized the gaming industry. The player, armed with weapons, is a space marine who faces level after level of demons and other denizens of hell. Dubbed a "mass-murder simulator" by critics, Doom is still considered to be public enemy number one, even ten years after its release. Despite the fact that this classic looks a bit old and almost archaic graphically, the Doom games are the most ported in history, even appearing on the Game Boy Advance and the Pocket PC.

Even though we'll probably never see this top ten list on *Late Night with David Letterman*, there's much we can learn about the potential dangers this kind of entertainment can have on our spiritual lives. But this is hardly a complete listing of games that should cause us to be concerned. Check out some of these games and the way the manufacturers describe them.

- *Warcraft III: Frozen Throne*

  There's a new hero for the "undead"—Crypt Lord. He can impale enemy units and then toss them into the air, which either kills them or stuns them when they land. Humans in this game have access to the Blood Mage Hero unit that can cast spells such as Flame Strike and Banish.

- *Grand Theft Auto: Vice City*

  An amazing cast of voice talent was assembled for GTA including *GoodFellas'* Ray Liotta, Joe Pantoliano from *The Sopranos*, Gary Busey, and adult-film star Jenna Jameson. The game is set in Miami, and these professional actors make the characters sing—shirtless jocks cruise by on roller skates, spandex-sporting hotties throw out lewd comments, and even the most innocuous character can say or do something that stops you in your tracks. It's filled with "exaggerated violence and seamy antics."

- *Blood Rayne*

  Behold agent Blood Rayne, half human and half vampire— all woman. In this game, the wickedly sexy heroine will seductively escort the player into the terrifying world of the occult.

- *Primal*

  The battle to save the outside world starts within as Jen Tate—a modern-day girl—faces the demons of an immortal realm and discovers her own supernatural origin.

- *Eternal Ring*

  A young magician is sent by his king to investigate the strange happenings on the Island of No Return, armed with his sword and natural talents as a sorcerer.

- *Neverwinter Nights: Shadows of Undrentide*

  This game contains approximately fifty spells, such as the gorgan that encases you in stone. Fantastic effects like the giant green fist of Bigby's Hand spells accompany many of these.

- *Warhammer*

A tabletop war game of fantasy battles played by two or more people where you get to build, paint, and develop your own players. Warhammer's probably the most popular fantasy role-playing game internationally, even though many would just call it a war game. You can play small-scale skirmish games involving twenty or thirty models per side, up to massed battles that pit armies of hundreds of models against each other. Rules that govern how the models move and fight are contained in the Warhammer rulebook. Some of the character pieces and armies for the game include Skaven, Hordes of Chaos, Tomb Kings, and Dark Shadows. Everything is in one place, from moving and shooting, to close assaults (vicious hand-to-hand combat), and even using vehicles and psychic powers.

Games like these are more than just entertainment. They entice kids through the attraction of supernatural powers of magic and sorcery and can become doorways for a teen's first steps into the occult. I'm not saying that all video and computer games are occultic, but you need to screen the games you allow in your home and weed out any that could tantalize your teen to the dark side.

COMMON THEMES AND CONTENT

The list of games we've looked at in this chapter is in no way complete. There are plenty of other games on the market just like these, plus there are new ones coming out all the time. But it does give us a pretty good idea of what's out there right now. Did you notice the themes and content found in the games we looked at? Check it out and see how you feel about them:

- psychic powers
- incantations and spells
- violence, gore, and murder
- magic and sorcerers
- demons
- the occult
- immoral sex
- vampires
- vulgar language
- assault and degradation of women

Before we go any further, STOP, step back from your teen's favorite game(s), and think for a few minutes about its themes and content. Is it similar to the list above? Now, I'm not trying to ruin anyone's fun, and I'm not against a healthy fantasy game. But is the game your teen playing the kind he or she can get emotionally and mentally wrapped up in? Do you want this kind of stuff influencing the way they think, feel, and act? And most importantly, what does God have to say about these things in the Bible?

You might be thinking, *Steve, only people who are unstable to begin with will commit violent acts, use spells, dabble in the occult, or commit a crime because of their involvement with fantasy role-playing games. And besides that, just because someone plays a game and is obsessed with it doesn't mean the game itself made them think or act a certain way.* There's a note of truth here, because there are usually several things that contribute to someone committing a heinous act. But the Bible makes it very clear that we are to guard our minds. Look at it this way: How much anthrax does it take to harm you? Just a tiny bit. Or what about the power of a sixty-second commercial to influence you to purchase something? In other words, it doesn't take much spiritual poison to throw us off the track spiritually and give the devil an opportunity to influence our thinking.

And remember, it's what we allow inside our hearts and minds that will greatly influence the way we live. Jesus put it this way: "A good person produces good deeds from a good heart, and an evil person produces evil deeds from an evil heart. Whatever is in your heart determines what you say" (Luke 6:45). Jesus reminds us that our speech and actions reveal our real underlying beliefs. What we allow inside us will come out in the way we live.

VALUE VS. DANGER

Another way to determine whether video and computer games are beneficial is to ask yourself, *Are there actually any real-life, real-world benefits to my teen playing RPGs?* You may have read stories of people who met while playing an MMORPG online and ended up getting married. That's a nice warm, fuzzy story, but I'm not convinced it's a good enough reason to spend multiple hours each day living an alternate life in a fantasy game world. Or ask yourself, *Does playing RPGs really have a positive influence on my teen's daily life and his or her interaction with others?* The issue isn't fantasy entertainment, it's playing healthy fantasy games—and being careful to guard yourself against getting desensitized to negative themes and content found in so many of the popular role-playing games.

The problem is that people who get involved with some RPGs actually lose track of what's reality and what's fantasy. Then they become desensitized to all kinds of evil, violence, and even the occult. A little bit of curiosity can lead to an unhealthy fascination and ultimately to an uncontrolled obsession.

Add to this the fact that we live in a society that increasingly rejects absolutes, and where fantasy and reality are constantly being blurred. Take, for example, what happened at the University of Arizona College of Nursing in Tucson. Three days before Halloween, three faculty members were shot to death in a classroom by a student who was failing classes. The gunman subsequently took his own life. Another scary part of this story was how students in the classroom first responded after the shooting. Many were quoted as saying, "Wow, what an awesome Halloween practical joke. The blood looked so real." It's unbelievable to think that college-age students could not tell the difference between fantasy and reality—even when it came to seeing someone murdered right in front of their eyes. Part of that is desensitization from having so much violence and gore in entertainment today.

A game by itself can't make you kill someone or commit a violent act, but it can influence your thinking and desensitize you to certain things. There are some fantasy role-playing games with healthier and more positive themes, but teens (and parents) must constantly be on their guard. By participating in some of these games, teens can open themselves up to be gradually seduced mentally and emotionally. Overexposure to evil characters, violence, sex, and occult themes can corrupt their values and open up their minds to demonic influence. Those involved with role-playing games can become much more accepting of evil, which could pave the way for the enemy to gain a foothold in their life and infiltrate their mind as they become more desensitized.

For many teenagers and adults alike, certain role-playing games are the first step into the world of the occult—similar in a way to gateway drugs like marijuana. Satan slowly sneaks in, attempting to distract, disappoint, and ultimately destroy. John 10:10 puts it this way: "The thief's purpose is to steal and kill and destroy." What's his objective? He wants to steal, kill and destroy our purity, the truth, our faith, our happiness and joy—basically anything and everything, including our relationship with Jesus.

And don't forget, just because I didn't list a specific game in this chapter doesn't mean it's okay for your teen (or you) to play it. Whether it's been out for a while, something that's just been released, or a game that will pop up in the future—use basic principles from the Bible to decide if it's something that God wants you to participate in and allow to influence your thinking.

But it's not just games such as those listed above that are seducing our kids into the darkness. It's also happening at school.

DEALING WITH DANGERS IN THE CLASSROOM

There is some interesting subject matter being taught in classrooms today. Many teachers say these materials and methods challenge a student's imagination and stretch their potential. Others say it's damaging to kids who are subjected to occultic teaching methods.

These teaching methods are a danger to our teens because they oppose biblical guidelines. For example:

Confluent education, which is compatible with the term *values clarification,* posits the equality of individual values, because according to confluent education, everyone has the wisdom of the universe within them. The idea is that this education will help each child discover his or her truth, since it teaches that there is no absolute truth. Confluent education not only teaches that there is no absolute truth, but also that sin is nonexistent, and therefore Jesus Christ and what He accomplished on the cross is unnecessary. Confluent education is dangerous because it leads kids to believe that they are divine and perfect. Being taught they are godlike, kids develop a false self-confidence.

Guided imagery in the classroom is dangerous because it teaches kids a way of dealing with problems that leaves God out of the picture. Guided imagery is a method like creative visualization-led meditation. It's designed to promote physical healing or attitudinal behavioral changes. Practitioners act as prompters and orally outline scenes and/ or give instructions on using imagery for self-help. It focuses the power of the mind on some aspect of the workings of the body in order to cause a real, positive response. It can also open them up to the "angel of light" (2 Corinthians 11:14). Satan and his servants can deceive us by appearing to be attractive.

Visualization is dangerous because it denies the lostness of all people and the impact sin has on human imagination (Genesis 6:5). When visualization is used in the classroom, students are taught to visualize ideal situations for their life as a step to realizing them.

Values clarification in the classroom is a menace because it denies the existence of moral absolutes from the Bible. Instead, each student is encouraged to come up with his or her own moral value system.

Eastern meditation in the classroom is perilous because kids are taught to empty their minds with the goal of attaining oneness with all things—a kind of "cosmic consciousness." Biblical meditation is much different because it always has the objective of filling the mind with the Word of God.

Globalism (an outlook or policy that is worldwide in scope—sometimes it's a euphemism for one-world government) is threatening because it is based on a monistic world view that promotes the unity of all humankind and all religious beliefs.

With the mental and spiritual well-being of our teens at stake, the real issue is not the good (but sometimes misguided) intentions of teachers and administrators. Rather we must ask, "What does God's Word say about such practices?" Deuteronomy 18:10–11 clearly forbids many of the methods we have been discussing: "For example, never sacrifice your son or daughter as a burnt offering. And do not let your people practice fortune-telling or sorcery, or allow them to interpret omens, or engage in witchcraft, or cast spells, or function as mediums or psychics, or call forth the spirits of the dead."

HOMEWORK FOR PARENTS

Perhaps you are a Christian parent whose teen attends a public school. How can you guard them and their fellow students against the subtle seduction of occultic materials and methods?

Paul's encouraging words in 1 Corinthians 16:13–14 are a good place to start: "Be on guard. Stand true to what you believe. Be courageous. Be strong. And everything you do must be done with love." It's important to keep these biblical principles in mind as you develop a strategy for handling the harmful influences impacting our educational system.

Here are some steps to consider for protecting your teens against harmful practices in the classroom and replacing harmful materials and methods with those that are more positive:

1. *Stay informed.* Most parents don't have a clue about the materials and methods used in the schools their teens attend. Contact your teen's school office and ask for permission to review the materials being used. If your request is denied, file a complaint with the district. Do your homework. Be able to cite the specific dangers of offensive materials and methods. Earn the right to be heard by being thorough, well-prepared, and positive.

2. *Get involved.* It's not enough for you to help with the band booster auction. Get into your child's classroom as a volunteer aide. Observe what is taking place. Inform the teacher and the administration if you notice any questionable practices. Yes, it will cost you some time and effort to get involved at this level. But you must ask yourself, *Do I want to pay now or later?*

3. *Gather support.* Seek out teachers, counselors, parents, pastors, and others who share your views. Develop a united task force and request a meeting with school or district administrators to discuss questionable materials and activities in the classroom. Be persistent.

4. *Take action when necessary.* If the administration rejects or ignores your requests, or if you have a one-sided, unproductive meeting, consider going to the school board. Prepare your thoughts, document your argument, and request everything in writing.

5. *Accept responsibility* for the parenting of your teen. If they are going to win in life, their most crucial need outside their personal relationship with Jesus Christ is strong parental support. You can only support your kids when you get personally involved in raising them. Their education isn't the school's job; it's your job. The school is merely helping you. And when the

school hinders more than it helps, it's your job to correct the problem.

Similarly, your teen's spiritual education and growth isn't the church's job; it's yours. The church may provide support, but it is your responsibility to help your teen develop a biblically based world view.

Let's do something before we lose an entire generation. Do not allow the complacency and relative truth of our society to subtly restrain you. There is too much at stake. We can't afford to allow the themes of despair, occultism, mutilation, and witchcraft to become entrenched in the vulnerable minds of our teens through our neglect. Jesus said, "It would be better to be thrown into the sea with a millstone tied around the neck than to face the punishment in store for harming one of these little ones. I am warning you!" (Luke 17:2–3).

CHAPTER 4:

TRENDS OF TODAY

WHAT WERE SOME of the popular trends when you were a teenager? Do you remember what styles were "in"? Or how about the blockbuster films and top-selling albums?

Let's take a brief look at some of the popular trends of today to bring you up-to-date.

FASHIONS FIT FOR THE FIRE

In the last fifty years teenagers have been famous for their unconventional clothes and hair, from the leather jackets and ducktails of the '50s to the bizarre punk styles of the '80s. For many of today's teens, clothing, makeup, and hairstyles are still outward signs of an inward struggle for acceptance and identity. But some of today's fashions seem to encourage a step into the darkness to meet these needs.

In many Southern California malls, there is a trendy shop geared for teens. Over 95 percent of the items in the store sport occultic or satanic symbols. They are embroidered or painted on belts, scarves, jewelry, T-shirts, ties, pants, hats, socks, buttons, and stickers. The stores are often packed with teens and preteens searching for the hottest "evil-looking" article to help them gain acceptance with the crowd at school. Even some of the major department stores have started carrying occultic fashions.

Wicca is also making a fashion-trend statement. You can now buy clothing with the word *Goddess* printed on it; there's the Earth Goddess collection of cosmetics; and there are even "potions" fragrances showing up in some of the hipper stores.

There are at least two dangers in allowing your teens to wear fashions decorated with satanic and occultic symbols. First, the symbols represent values and a lifestyle that is contrary to what the Bible teaches. Second, in their desperate attempt to change their lives and overcome the pain of day-to-day living, teens may decide to experiment with these symbols to see if there really is any power in them. Teens who play around with these things often find more than they bargained for.

Some teens like to dress in black. Some even go so far as to dye their hair black, wear pale makeup accented in dark colors, and paint their fingernails black. Kids who are obsessed with black may be mirroring an unhealthy inner fascination with darkness. Those who are caught up in these fads may be subconsciously crying out, "Please help me!" But be careful not to overreact; the key word here is *obsessed*. Black is also a fashionable color.

SCREAMS FROM THE SCREEN

When the movie *The Craft* was first released, it triggered a huge increase in the number of people contacting Wicca groups online. The film, about a modern-day coven of young witches, is about three high school outcasts who practice witchcraft but struggle to attain the kinds of results they want; they need a fourth member of the coven. That role is fulfilled by the new girl in town, Sarah Bailey. Sarah seems to be a normal high school student, yet we soon learn that she has a history of making things happen around her when she's upset, and that this problem has led to one suicide attempt in the past. The three resident weird girls at school soon recognize Sarah's inherent magickal abilities and bring her into their circle. The leader of the group is Nancy Downs, a tough, unstable girl who oozes attitude from every pore in her body. She has a much deeper interest in the uses of magick than her "sisters," Rochelle and Bonnie, and the fact that Sarah seems to have more in the way of magickal potential than she does gnaws away at her over time.

After first succeeding at a few parlor-trick types of magic, the girls put their powers to more serious use. Bonnie asks for the scars she was born with to be removed; Rochelle wants payback against a cruel, racist girl at school; and Sarah wants the creep of a guy she likes to fall in love with her. Nancy has larger ambitions, invoking the spirit of Manol and all his powers. (Or "Manon"—the fictitious name given to this spirit that supposedly represents the one beyond everything, or the All.) The spells begin to work, but they work a little too well, leading to some pretty significant internal troubles for the coven.

Charmed, another story about a coven of young female witches, has become a huge hit on the WB television network. The Halliwell sisters—Phoebe, Prue, and Piper—each have a big problem in life. Prue and Piper both have hard-to-please bosses, while Phoebe can't seem to keep a job. One day Phoebe starts playing with a Ouija board when it mysteriously spells out *attic.* Phoebe ventures up into the attic and finds a mysterious book labeled *The Book of Shadows* in a glowing chest. Phoebe reads a spell that releases the sisters' powers, and they discover that they're descendents of a line of female witches. Each one has a special ability—moving objects, stopping time, seeing the future—and they can also combine their abilities into the "Power of Three" to fight demons, warlocks, and other evil beings.

Do you remember *Sabrina, the Teenage Witch?* Sabrina Spellman thought she was a normal sixteen-year-old until her aunts—Hilda and Zelda—tell her that she is a witch, along with her whole family on her father's side. While preparing to get her witch's license, Sabrina ends up living with her aunts in Massachusetts. Sabrina gets into several scrapes as she tries to figure out how certain spells work.

Then there's the *Bewitched* movie starring Nicole Kidman and Will Ferrell. Based on the classic TV show from 1964–1972, *Bewitched* is a romantic comedy about an entire family of witches who are immortal. One member of the family is a beautiful witch named Samantha who marries a mortal husband and promises to give up her special powers— much to the disapproval of her relatives. These witchy relatives are constantly interfering in the marriage by using their magick in mischievous ways. And Samantha herself struggles with the temptation to use her magickal powers to get things done around the house.

How about Saturday morning television? Themes of witchcraft and sorcery can even be found in cartoons like *Sabrina, W.I.T.C.H., Scooby Doo,* and *Shaman King.*

No doubt the media has helped witchcraft gain a much bigger presence in society in the last few years. Wicca is everywhere! (We'll look more closely at the aspects and characteristics of Wicca beginning in chapter 5.)

A teen's naïve fascination with darkness veiled as entertainment may encourage further steps into the occult. Remind them of Philippians 4:8: "Fix your thoughts on what is true and honorable and right. Think about things that are pure and lovely and admirable. Think about things that are excellent and worthy of praise."

CHEMICAL CATASTROPHES

Drug and alcohol abuse has reached epidemic proportions in our society, especially among teens.

Teens generally use and abuse drugs and alcohol for two main reasons, besides the fact that their friends may be indulging: First, alcohol and/or drugs make them feel good. Everything about their lives is changing so rapidly that they are often filled with boredom, confusion, loneliness, alienation, and unhappiness. Intoxicating substances are enchanting and exhilarating, helping them dull the pain and pressure in their lives. An eleven-year-old cocaine addict said he had used drugs "so I wouldn't have to feel anymore."

Second, substance use gives kids a sense of security. The breakdown of the family and the uprooting that kids experience every couple of years as families move creates insecurity. Alcohol and drugs appear more dependable to them than family or friends, are there when kids need them, and work every time.

It's no coincidence that the rise in occultic activity among young people parallels the rise in substance abuse. There is a definite link between the two (although not every young person using drugs is necessarily involved in the occult). Satan's goal is to capture a child's mind. Mind-altering substances leave kids vulnerable to his control. A fifteen-year-old girl summed it up this way: "Taking drugs is like getting into a strange car with someone you don't know, who's going to take you down a road you've never been before."

I received a phone call from a mother who was filled with anxiety and pain. "Steve, you've got to help me," she pleaded. "I just found a loaded gun, a bag of narcotics, and an altar to Satan in my teenage son's bedroom. I don't know what to do." "How long have these things been in his room?" I asked. "I don't know," she said. "It's been months since I've been in his room or had a real conversation with him."

When I got off the phone with her, I headed to the large public high school I was set to speak at. When I arrived, the principal introduced himself and wanted to tell me a little bit about his school. "We have a great student body here at this school, Steve. We have very few kids who are sexually active and virtually no problems with drug or alcohol abuse." At first I thought the principal was kidding, but the look on his face told me that he naïvely believed what he had just said. I spend enough time on campuses each year to be able to pretty much pick kids out of the crowd who are struggling with various issues. I had to fight the temptation of wanting to drag this guy up into the bleachers and point out some teens who were struggling with chemical abuse.

Unfortunately, there are many parents like this mother and high school principal. They spend so little time with their teens that they are unaware of the symptoms of substance use and abuse. The more involved and communicative you are with your teen, the more you will protect him or her against the seduction of substances and the steps into darkness they encourage.

DANCING IN THE DARK

So much secular music today discusses all the problems in the world at present but never offers any solutions. There seems to be a core message of hopelessness and a lack of solid answers. If we listen to these messages long enough, we will start to believe them. And when you lose your hope, you'll do just about anything. We need to encourage our teens to carefully examine the philosophies songs are promoting. Colossians 2:8 says, "Don't let anyone lead you astray with empty philosophy and high-sounding nonsense that come from human thinking and from the evil powers of this world, and not from Christ."

There are also prominent themes of sex, violence, rebellion, suicide, and the occult in secular music. To see the effect these messages are having, all you have to do is pick up a magazine or watch the news. While music can't make you do something, it can become your philosophy of life. And those beliefs eventually shape your behavior. A nineteen-year-old girl in Florida, who shot and killed a German tourist, said her "inspiration to murder came from a rap song." Music is not the only thing causing these problems, but it's definitely one of the most important contributing factors. Music not only reflects the youth culture, it directs it as well.

Rap music is extremely popular today. Artists like 50 Cent, Nelly, Lil' Kim, and Jay-Z are just a handful of names that get tremendous airplay. And we can't look at this genre without mentioning Eminem. His lyrics are chock-full of dazzling escapades that delve into the mind of a violently warped and vulgar songwriter. Some say he has written some of the most demented lyrics ever recorded. "I do say things that I think will shock people," he says. "But I don't do things to shock people. I'm not trying to be the next Tupac, but I don't know how long I'm going to be on this planet. So while I'm here, I might as well make the most of it."[1]

But Eminem's not the only artist who tries to outrage people. Check out shock-rocker Marilyn Manson. No music discussion would be complete without mentioning the former Brian Warner, known for his ghastly cadaverous look with makeup and body piercing. In some cities, his concerts have drawn protests because of his controversial macabre lyrics and outrageous stage behavior. Manson's music encourages drug abuse, violence, hatred, death, and suicide.

I'm not saying that Eminem or Marilyn Manson are Satan worshipers, but can you see how subtly the devil is using their music—and that of many other artists—to promote his occultic lies? First Thessalonians 5:21 is a great example to remind us that we need to test everything we listen to musically against the truth of God's Word, no matter what the style of music: "Test everything that is said. Hold on to what is good." We need to equip our teens to be more selective in the music they listen to.

---

[1]*www.eminem.com*

SURFING THE WEB

As I write this chapter, there are well over one million hits for *Wicca* on Google—although I have noticed this figure changes almost daily. Internet resources on witchcraft are growing daily by the thousands. The Internet may be the source that has introduced more teens to Wicca than anything else. The world of witchcraft can be explored without ever leaving one's room. As parents, you may never notice a thing. Wiccan teens can connect with others just like them in a chat room or on a message board and discuss things that could end up in their Book of Shadows. (If you're not familiar with this term, take a quick look in the glossary at the back of the book.)

Pagan (see definition in glossary) and Wiccan spirituality has achieved an impressive online presence. This is really not surprising, as the Wiccan community often faces discrimination or harsh criticism in the real world but can present itself favorably in the anonymous slipstreams of cyberspace. Alternative thinkers can find a home both in cyberspace and in the old religion (witchcraft).[2]

Teens wishing to learn about witchcraft can take classes online through the Academy of Sorcery, work on a degree or certification at Working Witches, or attend the Church and School of Wicca. There's even a Web site that will cast spells for teens—100 percent satisfaction guaranteed. Luck, love, money—whatever you want. And there's tons of free stuff available for download or online ordering through thousands of Web sites.

HARRY POTTER AND FRIENDS

Even though the Internet has become so huge in size and influence, it still will never totally replace books—in Wiccan culture or with the culture in general. According to the *New York Times*, Wicca is the fastest-growing, most lucrative subject in publishing today.[3] And *Harry Potter* is right at the top of the list.

British novelist J. K. Rowling has turned her childhood fantasies into literary magic.[4] Her *Harry Potter* book series is selling millions of copies

[2]Carl McColman, *The Well-Read Witch* (Franklin Lakes, NJ: New Page Books, 2002), 249–250.
[3]Fiona Horne, *Pop! Goes the Witch* (New York, NY: The Disinformation Company, Ltd., 2004), 17.
[4]Raffaella Barker, "Harry Potter's Mum," *Good Housekeeping*, October 2000, 85.

and generating hundreds of millions of dollars in sales. The movies—based on the books—have a magic all their own. This bespectacled wizard, who attends Hogwarts School of Witchcraft and Wizardry, has exposed vast audiences to the world of witchcraft. With each book in the series, the story lines have gotten darker. But the line between fact and fiction has also been greatly blurred by Harry Potter. The Pagan Federation, which provides information on Paganism to counter misconceptions about the religion, has appointed a youth officer to deal with the flood of inquiries following the success of the book series.

Letters have been written addressed to Professor Dumbledore—fictitious Headmaster at fictitious Hogwarts—from real-life children and teens begging to be let into the school. It's like they want it to be true so badly, they've convinced themselves it's real.

Harry Potter has had a profound impact on the attitudes and behavior of this generation. Check out the following:

- British opticians have a young wizard to thank for a recent boom in business. Anticipating the opening of the movie *Harry Potter and the Sorcerer's Stone*, eye doctor's report 40% of children getting their eyes tested say they're doing it in hopes of being diagnosed with a need for glasses—just like Harry Potter's. Even those who don't have impaired vision are asking for plain glass spectacles.[5]
- Forget Tickle-Me Elmo dolls and Pokémon cards. The latest "must haves" for kids are . . . old-fashioned brooms? Brian Eddon, a British besom maker, reports that sales of his brooms have spiked in the U.K. since the release of the Harry Potter movie. "Children have seen [the brooms] in the film and ask their parents to buy them one," he says.[6]
- Fears that *Harry Potter* is promoting interest in witchcraft are being realized in Australia. Adelaide University says the books and movie have prompted the launch of a twelve-week course on witchcraft, covering everything from witches of the sixteenth century to present-day witch doctors in Africa. The course will be open to the public.[7]

[5]ABC World News Now, 11/6/01.
[6]*CNN.com*, 10/31/02.
[7]BBC News, 2/18/02.

- In Kansas, the Oskaloosa Public Library had planned to launch a reading program based on the *Harry Potter* books. An ad in *The Oskaloosa Independent* promoted the program as "Muggle Studies" for "aspiring young witches and wizards." But some residents were unhappy enough about the program that they convinced the library's board to cancel the event. Librarian Paula Ware said a small group of Oskaloosa residents thought the program would teach children about witchcraft. "They felt very threatened by the evil factor in the book," she told *The Lawrence Journal-World*.[8]

- A twenty-one-year-old woman from Madrid, Spain, set her house ablaze on July 9 while attempting to brew a potion like Harry Potter. Her concoction, composed of water, alcohol, oil and toothpaste, proved more flammable than magical, destroying half her home in the resultant conflagration.[9]

- British Association of Teachers and Lecturers (ATL) general secretary Peter Smith is worried that *Harry Potter* mania will encourage children to dabble in witchcraft. But he cautions against overreacting, urging parental involvement instead. "Increasing numbers of children are spending hours alone browsing the Internet in search of satanic Web sites," he says. "ATL is concerned that nobody is monitoring this growing fascination. . . . The *Harry Potter* movie will lead to a whole new generation of youngsters discovering witchcraft and wizardry. We welcome the values this will ingrain, focusing on good triumphing over evil. Though it is important not to overreact to this fun and entertaining phenomenon, the risks are clear."[10]

Am I trying to say that if a teen reads a *Harry Potter* book they will get involved in witchcraft or the occult? No. But I am saying that it just could be a doorway into Wicca. The Bible warns us not to give the devil a foothold (Ephesians 4:27). Remember, the spiritual battle is essentially a battle for our minds and hearts. The last thing our teens or we should do is give the enemy a chance—however large or small—to influence our thinking. Review the illustrations above. If reading a

---

[8]Associated Press/Fox News Online, 6/13/01.
[9]Reuters, 7/9/03.
[10]BBC News Online, 11/5/01.

Harry Potter book or watching a movie can influence these kinds of attitudes, there is definitely the capacity for other more serious desires to develop. Teens need to know how subtle the enemy is and that the battle is real. While speaking at summer camp in northern California, I went into a Wicca store called 13. As I looked around the store I saw many of the tools and potions mentioned in the *Harry Potter* books— but this stuff was for real.

Carl McColman, author of *The Aspiring Mystic,* has put together a book called *The Well-Read Witch* to help anyone interested in finding the best books to read on Wicca. McColman reviews over four hundred books in his paperback and also provides a basic overview of Wiccan spirituality. Llewellyn Publishers in St. Paul, Minnesota, is one of the largest producers of books on witchcraft, releasing dozens of new books each year. *Teen Witch: Wicca for a New Generation,* written by bestselling author Silver Ravenwolf, is one of the most popular books they have published. It's sold more than any other book in their ninety-five-year history.[11] There are some people who call Silver Ravenwolf— Wiccan Priestess and the Director of the International Wiccan/Pagan Press Alliance—"Mama Silver" because "she cares so much about those who read her books."[12] Her writing covers everything from spells for homework and dating to all you need to know to become a pentacle-wearing, spell-casting authentic witch.

They also publish Scott Cunningham's book *Wicca: A Guide for the Solitary Practitioner.* It's probably one of the most widely read books on Wicca and has sold over four hundred thousand copies. Cunningham tells his readers that Wicca is varied and multifaceted and, as in every religion, the Wiccan experience is one shared with deity alone. "I write based on my experiences and the instruction I have received to practice Wicca."[13]

Llewellyn has developed quite a catalog of fiction and nonfiction witchcraft books for teens, including titles like *Spellcraft for Teens—A Magickal Guide to Writing and Casting Spells,* the *Witchy Day Planner,* and *Teen Goddess: How to Look, Love and Live Like a Goddess.*

---

[11]"Teens & Wicca—Why (and how many) youth are drawn to Wicca," *www.religioustolerance. com.*

[12]Silver Ravenwolf, *Teen Witch* (St. Paul, MN: Llewellyn Publications, 2000), xv.

[13]Scott Cunningham, *Wicca: A Guide for the Solitary Practitioner* (St. Paul: Llewellyn Publications, 2003), xi-xii.

Walk into a bookstore and you'll find dozens of books on the same topic by people like Gary Cantrell, Phyllis Curott, Jamie Wood, and even celebrities like Fiona Horne. You'll even find *The Complete Idiot's Guide to Wicca and Witchcraft.*

There's also been a huge increase in the number of local publications in various areas. I picked up a copy of a quarterly pagan magazine called *The Community Seed.* It claims to be an organization supporting pagans and other earth-based spiritualists through community service, publications, events, and other ritual celebrations. They define a pagan as "one who follows their own unique spiritual path, honoring both male and female aspects of deity, and in tune with their connection to the Earth, the Elements and the turning of the seasons."

All of these publications and more are giving Wicca "an extreme makeover" and helping it to "come out of the closet." When you take into consideration the huge exposure witchcraft is getting on the Internet and in the media with TV shows and movies, you see it's got a whole new look for a whole generation. Wicca appears to have a new credibility and an ability to seemingly compete head-on with other faiths.

WHAT THE BIBLE HAS TO SAY

If you're determined to help protect your teen from witchcraft and the occult, as well as help him or her grow in their relationship with Jesus and want the very best He has to offer, encourage your teen to take the Bible seriously so he or she will practice obeying it in every dimension of their life—including entertainment and recreation.

To help you with this challenge, let's check out biblical guidance to help your teen make godly decisions about the content and themes in games, music, movies, TV shows, and Web sites. The goal is to help them make their own decision about those things based on the standards of God's Word.

Evil

> Don't get sidetracked; keep your feet from following evil. (Proverbs 4:27)

> Furthermore, since they did not think it worthwhile to retain

the knowledge of God, he gave them over to a depraved mind, to do what ought not to be done. They have become filled with every kind of wickedness, evil, greed and depravity. They are full of envy, murder, strife, deceit and malice. (Romans 1:28–29 NIV)

Dear friend, do not imitate what is evil but what is good. Anyone who does what is good is from God. Anyone who does what is evil has not seen God. (3 John 11 NIV)

God has a plan and purpose for each one of us. He has a pathway of life that will give us the greatest amount of happiness and satisfaction. But that means we need to stay on God's pathway and not get sidetracked on detours, including evil in any form. God feels so strongly about the hazards of evil that He doesn't even want us to imitate it.

Magick, Spells, and Sorcery

Do not let your people practice fortune-telling or sorcery, or allow them to interpret omens, or engage in witchcraft, or cast spells, or function as mediums or psychics, or call forth the spirits of the dead. (Deuteronomy 18:10–11)

Blessed are those who wash their robes so they can enter through the gates of the city and eat the fruit from the tree of life. Outside the city are the dogs—the sorcerers, the sexually immoral, the murderers, the idol worshipers, and all who love to live a lie. (Revelation 22:14–15)

The Bible leaves no room for doubt where God stands on the use of magick, spells, or sorcery of any form. He wants us to have nothing to do with them. Why? Because they are harmful to us, and because when embraced, they have power to harm our relationship with Him. When we're having "fun" doing something, it's easy to ignore the potential dangers. Remember, God is for you and always wants the best for you. He demonstrated this to us in a way no one else ever could— by the death of His only Son, Jesus, on the cross.

Immorality and Sex

Run away from sexual sin! No other sin so clearly affects the body as this one does. For sexual immorality is a sin against your own body. (1 Corinthians 6:18)

Let there be no sexual immorality, impurity, or greed among you. Such sins have no place among God's people. (Ephesians 5:3)

So put to death the sinful, earthly things lurking within you. Have nothing to do with sexual sin, impurity, lust, and shameful desires. Don't be greedy for the good things of this life, for that is idolatry. (Colossians 3:5)

Coarse Language and Swearing

Obscene stories, foolish talk, and coarse jokes—these are not for you. Instead let there be thankfulness to God. (Ephesians 5:4)

But now is the time to get rid of anger, rage, malicious behavior, slander, and dirty language. (Colossians 3:8)

Murder and Violence

Do not murder. (Exodus 20:13)

You have heard that the law of Moses says, "Do not murder. If you commit murder, you are subject to judgment" (Matthew 5:21).

Good people enjoy the positive results of their words, but those who are treacherous crave violence. (Proverbs 13:2)

The Lord examines both the righteous and the wicked. He hates everyone who loves violence. (Psalm 11:5)

Let slanderers not be established in the land; may disaster hunt down men of violence. (Psalm 140:11 NIV)

So much of the world's attempt to amuse and entertain our teens leads them into the darkness. That's why it's so important to equip them with God's Word that can "turn on the light" in the darkness.

PREPARING FOR DANGER AHEAD

In 1922, Adolf Hitler began his national youth movement. He knew that if he could control the minds of young people he could control an entire generation. By 1932, the Hitler Youth had more than one hundred thousand members, and history records the appalling results of this madman's influence on those under his control.

This is the same strategy Satan has been using for centuries. The growing number of those getting involved in the occult is just another facet of his effort to seduce and control an entire generation. Let's rescue our teens by helping them prepare their minds for action (1 Peter 1:13). Remember: The occult and witchcraft are deeply ingrained in every level of our culture. We need to help our teens recognize Satan's subtle counterfeits and develop a Christ-centered, biblically based world view.

How can we accomplish this? Here are a few suggestions:

Monitor what they watch and listen to from the entertainment world: movies, music, and TV shows. Be aware of the games they play and what they read for recreational purposes. Also monitor closely where they go on the Internet. Talk to them about how God's truth applies to the concepts being presented in the media. Help them understand Satan's subtle attempts to seduce them through entertainment.

Take an active interest in their schoolwork and homework assignments. Be aware of what they are being taught.

Encourage them in their personal relationship with Jesus Christ. Pray daily for their mental, physical, spiritual, and emotional well-being. Help them develop a lifestyle that pleases God and obeys His Word. Equip them to answer the great rationalization of our day: "Everybody's doing it; why shouldn't I? Everybody's following their own set of rules; why shouldn't I?" Help them understand that they have the freedom to choose and that the best choice is to obey God.

Finally, and most importantly, provide a positive, godly example of living by God's truth on a daily basis. Being a godly example doesn't require you to be perfect, but it does require that you be genuine and authentic in your faith. Are you an obedient, loving, forgiving follower of Christ seven days a week, or only on Sundays?

Being a good example involves allowing your teen to see how you handle failure as well as success. When you make a mistake or don't have all the answers, admit it. When you lash out at your teen with a harsh attitude or word, apologize and ask his or her forgiveness. And be careful to "walk what you talk."

One Wednesday night while serving as a youth pastor in Los Angeles, I gave what I thought was an incredible Bible study to the youth group on the topic of building one another up. I challenged them to evaluate every word and action with the question, "Does this build up or edify?"

The following Saturday I was working with some of the teens from the group during a church workday. We had just finished cleaning the hallway in the Sunday school building when two guys ran out of a classroom and carelessly spilled hundreds of tiny plastic beads all over the floor. "You dummies! Look at what you just did!" I barked.

The youth group responded in perfect unison, "Steve, does that build up or edify?" Busted! I suddenly realized that my actions carried at least as much weight with them as my words.

It's little things like these that your kids will notice. If they see a gap between what you say and what you do, they will assume that a counterfeit lifestyle is the norm. But as they watch you recognize and dismiss Satan's counterfeits and embrace God's truth, they will learn to do the same.

As we continue to expose Satan's schemes, remember: No matter how many dark doorways beckon to your teens, Christ is the ultimate door to freedom. Your job is not to try to eliminate the darkness in your teen's life, you are simply to turn on the light of truth. In a sense, it doesn't really matter how the lie approaches your child. It may come from a TV show, movie, Web site, or even a demonic spirit in his room. In any event, you must help him dwell on "whatever is true" (Philippians 4:8 NIV). As you do, the light will overpower the darkness and the enemy's seduction will fail.

CHAPTER 5:

WHAT'S THE APPEAL?

SILVER RAVENWOLF HAS BEEN married for nineteen years and is a mother of four children. She says she's an average mom who worries about the same things other parents of teens worry about—drugs, strange ideas they come up with, sexual desires, fast cars, raging hormones, and a steady flow of cash from her bank account. Oh, I almost forgot—Silver is also one of the most famous witches in the United States today. And she's written a book to help teens through the tough times of growing up.

In her introduction for parents in her book *Teen Witch: Wicca for a New Generation*, she writes: "As you will understand when you read this book, witchcraft isn't something you need to worry about. Celebrate that your child seeks empowerment. If you feel that the Craft is still against your belief system after you've read the book, don't panic. I've written this book so that your teen (or you) can take any of the techniques herein and use them in your own religious background."[1]

Wicca almost sounds too good to be true—for teens *and* their parents.

So what is Wicca and what's the attraction? Why do so many teens seem to be drawn to Wicca? There's no real accurate method of estimating the number of Wiccan youth in North America. However, you can see just how big this "religion" is with teens by looking at the

---

[1]Ravenwolf, *Teen Witch: Wicca for a New Generation*, xiv.

number of books published, the number of Web sites and listings that are growing daily, and the media attention. I've noticed a huge increase in the number of teens who e-mail or call our ministry regarding Wicca in the last couple of years.

The teenage years tend to typically be a time of spiritual searching. Some teens will even abandon the religion of their parents in hopes of finding a belief system that better suits them. And for teens today, Wicca appears to offer a lot of fascinating qualities. Let's look at some:

TOLERANCE

Many teens are turned off by what they view as discrimination within some conservative Christian churches when it comes to things like sexual orientation, religious beliefs, and marital status. Teens see Wicca as being much more tolerant and accepting of diversity.

ENVIRONMENTALLY CONCERNED

Wiccans have strong beliefs about respecting and caring for the earth itself and the entire species of plants and animals. You will see in this chapter that they feel very connected to the earth and cycles of nature. And they completely reject what the Bible teaches in Genesis 1:28: "God blessed them and told them, 'Multiply and fill the earth and subdue it. Be masters over the fish and birds and all the animals.'"

They believe that humanity should live in cooperation with creation.

FLEXIBLE AND PERSONAL INVOLVEMENT

Some teens don't like the way church is practiced today. They feel that it's too much of a spectator event. They want more direct participation rather than watching the pastor performing rituals—it's the experience they see as lacking. In Wicca, not only do they have the opportunity to perform rituals solo or with a coven, they can even create rituals of their own—something that's unheard of in churches.

They can perform their rituals any place on the planet—indoors or outdoors, at any time of the year, day or night. Teens can also concentrate on whatever part of Wicca that interests them; they can emphasize spells or other forms of divination. It's totally up to them.

POWER

Initially a lot of teens are attracted to Wicca because of its power. They want to feel special and gain control of their lives through spells, incantations, and other mystical tools. This quest for power is heightened as a result of what they see in movies and TV about witchcraft.

NO LIST OF "THOU SHALL NOTS"

Wicca has a single, universal rule of behavior: the Wiccan Rede. We will look at this more later on in this chapter, but it basically means you can do whatever you want as long as you don't perceive it to harm anyone or yourself. This would include things like premarital sex and homosexuality. But *perception* is an unstable ground to walk on, as each individual's definition and idea of what harm is, is different. Each person's perception then becomes the ultimate standard. This question needs to be answered: Is there any worth to these types of values?

SEXUAL EQUALITY

In most Wiccan traditions, equality between the sexes is a common principle. Men and women are both viewed as having a male and female side, with the chore of balancing the two. They see this balance as being necessary everywhere in the universe. Wiccans tend to see the female principle as being very powerful and sometimes even more important than the male. This is appealing to teens who reject what they view as male domination in many Christian denominations. This is an important issue to deal with, and we will look at how Jesus really felt about women in chapter 6.

IMPROVED VISIBILITY AND PUBLIC PERCEPTION

Wicca seems to be everywhere—and it's become more socially acceptable than ever before. We have become culturally desensitized to the evil and dangerous witch. For example, look at movies like *The Craft* or TV shows like *Sabrina, the Teenage Witch, Buffy the Vampire Slayer*, and *Charmed*, one episode of which was titled "Something Wicca This Way Comes." These programs aren't necessarily about Wicca, but they certainly portray female witches in a positive light.

In the U.S. and Canada, Wiccans have become more vocal and demanding about their constitutionally guaranteed religious freedom. Wicca is getting more media attention than ever, as a result of TV documentaries and even public issues, like Wiccans in the military and Wiccan jewelry (pentacles) on high school campuses.

Once considered a weird religion of default for castoffs, losers, and social misfits, it's now attracting university intellectuals, the "cool" people, and quite a few kids who go to church. Wicca is the religion of witchcraft and the practice of folk magick.[2] *Magick,* spelled with a *k,* distinguishes the belief in using the "universe's energy" for spiritual purposes from the magical illusions performed by entertainers. It's got big appeal with teens and is showing up everywhere in pop culture.

The more books I read about Wicca and the more I study it, the harder it becomes to define. It's like trying to nail applesauce to the wall! You can ask ten different people on a high school campus about Wicca and you'll get fifty different explanations of what it is and how to practice it. No wonder it's so easy to get confused.

Whether it's practiced solo or with a group, Wicca is forever changing, and it's very personal in the way it's practiced. That's part of the appeal— you can pick and choose what you want to believe and come up with your own "brand" of Wicca that works right just for you. There is no one right way to practice the craft. The religion is what you make of it.[3]

Let's see if we can cut through the confusion and get a basic understanding of what Wicca is and how it got started. We'll also look at what Wiccans believe and how it compares to Christianity.

WHAT IS WICCA?

Wicca is a complicated, contemporary religion that is often associated with occultism, neo-paganism, and witchcraft. If you're confused about these terms, check out the glossary in Appendix C for some definitions. Wicca, also known as witchcraft or the Craft of the Wise, is a centuries-old religion. It emphasizes worship of the earth, all living creatures, and both the god and goddess.

Sounds a bit confusing that Wicca can be both contemporary and

---

[2]Cunningham, *The Truth About Witchcraft Today,* 2.
[3]Ravenwolf, 8.

centuries old, doesn't it? Wicca is an interesting religious model. Its core beliefs are the same today as they were centuries ago—they've just been repackaged for the twenty-first century, giving them a contemporary look and feel. Because Wicca is a build-as-you-go, flexible belief system, it's constantly fusing together the old with the new. And it fits perfectly with the human heart's desire to be free from restrictions and outside control.

Wiccans may be female or male, of any age or race. They may meet in groups of up to fifty or more, in cozy covens of thirteen or less, or worship the god and goddess alone. Though most speak English, they may call the deities in Spanish, French, Welsh, Swedish, Scottish Gaelic, German, Dutch, or in many other languages. As a religion, Wicca exists throughout Europe, in all fifty of the United States, in Central and South America, in Australia and Japan, and elsewhere.[4]

At the heart of Wicca is a central rule called the Rede, which says, "An ye harm none, do what ye will." (A copy of the entire poem can be found in Appendix B.) Basically, witches have the total freedom to do whatever seems right to them, as long as they don't harm themselves or anyone else.[5] But this is a bit confusing. Think about it: If there are no absolutes in Wicca, then your definition and mine of what it means to "harm someone" could be totally different and yet both right. It doesn't make logical sense.

For example, the decision to be sexually active before marriage is not prohibited or discouraged in Wicca. Teens need only make their decision based on an investigative process, which determines the potential for harm to either party. In some circumstances premarital sex can be seen as a positive moral activity as long as precautions are being taken to avoid diseases like STDs, pregnancy, and possible negative effects on the relationship.

Wiccans believe they create the universe in which they live; therefore, their magick will have an effect on that universe. When following the Rede, Wiccans can work whatever magick or spell they feel is necessary or appropriate. They claim they'll never use these actions to cause distress or harm to come to others in any way that those individuals would not bring on themselves by their own actions.

The Threefold Law is another closely related rule, which teaches that

---

4Cunningham, 4.
5Ibid.

anything you do will come back to you three times over. For example, if a witch casts a spell against someone, it will come back to that person with three times the power. This is the Wiccan concept of karma.

Whether someone calls himself or herself a witch, god and goddess worshiper, or a Wiccan, there are some things they have in common. To begin with, they all hope to get results by worshiping nature or using spiritual forces. But keep in mind that Wicca and Satanism is not the same thing. Most witches would say that they don't even believe in the devil or accept the concept of "absolute evil." They believe that to give evil a name is to give it power.[6] Because Wiccans say they don't believe in the devil, they get offended if anyone compares Wicca to Satanism (worshiping the devil). Nevertheless, at their very core Wicca and Satanism are the same—they both reject the truth as found in Jesus and in His Word, following the same lie that was started at the beginning of human history. Adam and Eve (see Genesis 3) also chose to disobey God and try to live without Him.

Wiccans say that Satan is just something Christians made up. But if you study the history of religion, you'll find the concept of Satan in many ancient belief systems. Take Manichaeism, for example. It was an ancient religion started by a Persian sage named Mani (born about A.D. 215). Part of the doctrine of Manichaeism includes a dualistic division of the universe into opposing realms of good and evil. The light (spirit) was led by God, and the darkness (matter) was led by Satan. This same type of tradition can be found in other religions like Judaism and even Islam.

But there's a distinction we need to make between other religious views of Satan and those of Christianity. In religions with dualism, the devil and God are equals; Christian teaching says they're not. The Bible teaches that Satan is a created being—a fallen angel—who is limited in his abilities and power, while God is all-powerful without any limitations. Because God is holy, He had to respond in a way consistent with His perfect moral nature.

A big part of the devil's strategy in spiritual warfare is deception. Satan even disguises himself as an "angel of light" (2 Corinthians 11:14). Satan and his demons can deceive us by appearing to be attractive, moral, and good. Think about the appeal of Wicca and all the "good

---

[6]Ravenwolf, 8.

things it stands for." But you may say, "Wiccans don't believe in the devil." The Bible is very clear that Satan not only exists but that he is also more than just an impersonal "force." You can say you don't believe in him, but that doesn't change the reality of his existence.

In the movie *Constantine*, Keanu Reeves plays a jaded private eye (John Constantine) with a knack for seeing things from a terrifyingly spiritual point of view. Angela Dodson, a skeptical policewoman played by Rachel Weisz, hires him to solve the mysterious suicide of her twin sister. While she declares, "I don't believe in the devil," Constantine insists, "Well, you should—he believes in you."

People are drawn to the craft for many reasons. Some just feel different from others or they feel a special kinship with animals—sometimes stronger than what they feel with humans. Others see Wicca as powerful or glamorous. Those involved in Wicca claim to have a depth of power far greater than is apparent to the average person. This power is drawn from several sources including the All (the god and the goddess), elements, ancestors, and angels. Witches use their own power—the power of the mind—to reveal what they need. According to those involved in Wicca, everybody has the power, but most people don't use it—sometimes because they're afraid. It's from this unused power of the mind, claim Wiccans, that abilities such as clairvoyance, telekinesis, and extrasensory perception (ESP) are found. We'll talk more about power in another chapter.

A big part of the allure of Wicca is being able to choose your own deity. This is especially appealing to anyone who's become dissatisfied with the structure and practices of mainstream religions.

WHAT DO WICCANS BELIEVE?

There are a couple of things to keep in mind before we look at what Wiccans believe. First, not all witches are religious. Second, Wicca is a very individualistic and experiential religion with a lot of emphasis on personal responsibility. For example, there's no need to confess sin and receive forgiveness from an outside "authority." Instead, Wiccans are supposed to own up to their actions, admit their mistakes, and make things right wherever they can.

Most Wiccans refuse to submit to any centralized authority and are against any organized belief system. Instead, they build their own religion by mixing and matching various views and practices. Wicca, like other neopagan religions, draws heavily on experience, so truth is relative. They're convinced that the only way you can know truth is through a kind of sixth sense or feelings. There are no absolutes. But there are some basic beliefs that are held sacred by all Wiccans out of which come the individual practices and traditions.

Wicca is a religion built around worship of two deities: the goddess and the god. According to Wiccan belief, before the creation of the earth, the All existed. This female spirit was all alone so she created her other half—the male spirit. And even though they were two spirits, they were one, and gave birth to the universe. They made the stars, moons, solar systems, and planets. While on the earth they made water, land, plants, animals, and people.

The All is both female and male—equals—and from them came the seeds of life. The god and goddess chose the sun and the moon to remind us of their presence. The sun is the physical symbol for the god, and the moon is the physical symbol for the goddess. The goddess is the female force, that portion of the ultimate energy source that created the universe. She is all-woman, all-fertility, all-love.[7] The god is the male force, the other half of the primal divine energy acknowledged by Wiccans. He is all-man, all-fertility, all-love.[8]

Wicca is grounded in worship of the earth, which is seen as an expression of the mother goddess and her companion, the horned god. Both of these deities manifest themselves in nature. Wiccans see the earth as a living goddess who blesses us and must be nurtured and cared for in return.[9] They believe that the goddess dwells in every single thing—in trees, rocks, raindrops, and even inside of you. In many ways, Wicca is similar to the nature religions mentioned in the Bible, where many gods were worshiped and religions mixed, like the fertility religions of Canaan (1 Kings 14:22–24).[10]

Wiccans also choose the form of deity that they work with based on their personal preferences and what they want to work on. For example,

[7]Cunningham, 72.
[8]Ibid., 75.
[9]Michele Morgan, *Simple Wicca* (Berkeley: Conari Press, 2000), 8.
[10]Craig S. Hawkins, *Goddess Worship, Witchcraft and Neo-Paganism* (Grand Rapids: Zondervan Publishing House, 1998), 8–11.

if they need to attract some loving energy, they might choose to call on the Greek goddess Aphrodite. Or if they have a big exam coming up, they might invoke Sarasvati, the Hindu goddess of language and wisdom. Wiccans can choose from lots of different gods and goddesses and traditions. Naming god is all about choosing what works for a witch based on the things that they identify with, relate to, like, and love. Michele Morgan, in her book *Simple Wicca*, says, "The beauty of the Wiccan path lies in the freedom to create your own personal experience of worship. No doctrine dictates who or what the god or goddess must be; rather, there are ancient and symbolic descriptions of their energies, and essences. The rest is, happily, up you. Do you desire a god who is tough or tender? Do you picture him bronze-skinned or fair? Is your goddess slender, or plump like the fruit swelling on the vine, with hair as golden as the September wheat fields?"[11] Not only do Wiccans have the complete freedom to choose whatever god they want to worship, but they work with the deities rather than beg for help from them.

When Wiccans first start practicing the craft, deities from different cultures—Greek, Roman, Hindu, Egyptian, Buddhist, Celtic, and others—shouldn't be mixed and matched. Instead, it's recommended that a witch learn all he or she can from one pantheon, and then they can branch out and learn how deities from different systems relate to one another.

A pantheon is the collection of all the different deities from one specific culture or tradition; Wiccans are encouraged to read up on the pantheon that appeals to them, an appeal usually connected to a person's needs at a particular time. Here are a few examples of various gods from the traditions mentioned above:

Greek

Athena. The goddess of wisdom is a beautiful and serious young woman. Because she is a warrior, she wears a breastplate and helmet and carries a lance and shield.

Eros. The god of sexual attraction often carries a lyre or a bow and quiver of arrows.

---

[11]Morgan, 30.

Roman

Fortuna. The goddess of fortune and fate carries a rudder from a ship, a sphere, and a wheel.

Janus. The god of beginnings and the guardian of doorways can see the inside and outside of all things at the same time.

Hindu

Ganesha. The elephant-headed god is the overcomer of obstacles. In his four arms he carries roses, a piece of his broken tusk, a bowl, and a thorn.

Lakshmi. The goddess of fortune and beauty is golden, always beautifully dressed, and sits on a lotus blossom.

Egyptian

Hathor. The goddess of love, beauty, and pleasure is a woman with the horns of a cow.

Osiris. The god of fertility and resurrection takes the form of a mummy with the head of a living man.

Buddhist

Maitreya. The future Buddha has the form of a man holding a flower and wearing a headdress.

Quan yin. The goddess of mercy will protect you from danger. Newlyweds often pray to her for fertility.

Celtic

Ogma. The god of language and inspiration takes the form of a wise old man.

Brigid. The goddess of craftspeople, inspiration, and healing has enormous strength and can help you endure hardship.

The Days of Power—the sacred holidays that make up the Wiccan calendar—come from the earliest observances of seasons and cycles. In the craft it's called the Wheel of the Year (see Appendix D). The image of an ever-turning wheel—the constancy of change, the flow of season into season, and humankind's inseparable relationship with the earth—is symbolic of the Wiccan view of life.[12]

---

[12]Ibid., 44.

Wiccans celebrate these eight main holidays, or *Sabbats,* all centered on the solar cycles, and occurring at the time of natural events associated with the change of seasons. (These are defined and explained in the book's appendix.) At least once per month witches also celebrate an *esbat,* a Wiccan moon ritual when the goddess is honored. An esbat is typically celebrated on a full moon, but it can be celebrated on any other phase of the moon. They are times for Wiccans to draw on their energy and do magick. According to Wiccans, each one of these celebrations happens at a time of heightened interaction between the supernatural and the natural worlds.[13]

Before we look at the Wiccan holidays, here are some definitions that will be of help in this process.

Solstice: One of the two points on the ecliptic at which its distance from the celestial equator is greatest and which is reached by the sun each year about June 21 or 22 and December 21 or 22.

Equinox: Either of the two times each year when the sun crosses the equator and the day and night are everywhere of equal length— about March 21 and September 23.

Ecliptic: The great circle of the celestial sphere that is the apparent path of the sun among the stars or of the earth as seen from the sun.

The Greater Sabbats

Samhain (pronounced SOW-wen, or sah-VEEN)—October 31. The Witch's New Year and the primary Sabbat from which all others flow. It also marks the death of the lord. Witches hold celebrations to honor the dead.

Imbolc (pronounced IM-bolk)—February 2. Sometimes called Candlemas, it's the time when Wiccans celebrate the renewing fertility of the earth. The goddess is seen as recovering from childbirth and the god is a small child.

Beltane (pronounced BEL-tayne)—April 30. The god has reached manhood; he and goddess (lord and lady) unite in a handfasting—a Wiccan marriage ceremony in which a couple (a man and a woman, two men, or two women) is joined together for as long as their love will last. If they decide that they no longer love each other, they can

---

[13]Sarah Hinlicky, "Witch Path Would You Choose?" *www.boundless.org,* 1999.

part. By uniting in a handfasting, the god and goddess help bring life and new growth to the earth.

Lughnassah (pronounced LOO-mus-uh)—August 1 or 2. It's also called Lammas (pronounced LAM-mahs), which means "loaf mass," and marks the beginning of the fall harvest. It celebrates the grain spirit—"a great provider." It represents the Wiccan Thanksgiving.

The Lesser Sabbats

Yule (pronounced YOOL)—December 21. Winter solstice. It is seen as the time when the god (lord) is reborn and light begins to return to earth. Wiccans celebrate by exchanging gifts and burning a Yule log.

Ostara (pronounced oh-STAR-ah)—March 21. Spring equinox. In Wiccan tradition, the god and goddess (lord and lady) are seen as young and innocent and begin to wonder about each other. A Wiccan celebration might include decorated eggs—some even have an egg hunt and enjoy chocolate bunnies.

Litha (pronounced LEE-tha)—June 21. Summer solstice. This is the time of the year when the god and goddess (lord and lady) are at their peak and everything is green and growing. Witches celebrate the strength of the god in all his glory and zeal. This is sometimes called Midsummer.

Mabon (pronounced MAY-bon)—September 21. Fall equinox. Wiccans celebrate the last fruits of the year in a sort of harvest festival. The god is weakening and preparing for his death on Samhain, and the goddess is already beginning to mourn his loss.

With some of these holidays, the date changes each year because of the solstices and equinoxes. This is a very simple outline of the Sabbats. The actual rituals can be much more intricate and elaborate, honoring the god and goddess.

Reincarnation

Wiccans believe in reincarnation, which deepens their need to "learn from all experiences." They believe there's no actual heaven or hell, but instead a place called Summerland, where they believe the soul goes after dying to wait for a new physical form. While there, Wiccans believe their spirit thinks about the life it just lived, what it learned, and where it will come back next. Then, before each soul leaves Summerland it will decide who it wants to be when it comes back and what lessons it will learn in the next lifetime. According to Wiccans, if a soul doesn't want to reincarnate right away, it can become a spirit guide. Ultimately, once a spirit has learned all it's supposed to learn and perfected this knowledge, it will be reunited and absorbed into the All.

Spells

Spell-casting and magick are a vital part of Wicca. Spells are seen as symbolic acts performed in an altered state of consciousness in order to cause a desired change. Spell-casting is a form of visualization also known as "guided imagery" or "mind over matter." *The Teen Spell Book* says that spells and tools of the craft are only as powerful as the emotions they raise inside of you.[14] For example, if a Wiccan believes that the color blue means courage, then it will call forth that ability. Wiccans use spells primarily to discipline the mind and create the fulfillment of their wishes. *The Teen Spell Book* goes on to say that because they are so powerful, Wiccans must be very careful before they direct their intent or focus on anything.

Spell-casting also involves a number of ritual steps. A witch would start by casting a circle, then purifying and cleansing him or herself and any other participants. Following this they must ask for protection from the four directions and their guides, give an offering to the god and goddess, and set up the cone of power.

Sacred Text

A basic sacred text for many witches is something they call a Book of Shadows. It's named such because magick works outside of time and space and in the "in-between" space of light and darkness, sounds and silences—the shadows. Plus, in the past witches would have to gather for their celebrations or exchange information in the shadows. A Book of Shadows is a spiritual diary that contains spells, spiritual thoughts, as well as formulas for the proper preparation of potions. This diary is where witches keep track of their feelings, experiences, and lessons they've learned. Anything and everything related to their craft experience can be put in their Book of Shadows. It's like a personal reference book.

---

[14]Jamie Wood, *The Teen Spell Book* (Berkeley: Celestial Arts, 2001).

THE HISTORY OF WICCA

There's no real agreement as to the roots of Wicca. Some say Wicca is a direct religious descendant of the ancient Druids and Celts. Others claim it is much more modern—having been started within the last fifty or sixty years. Still other people believe it's at least twenty-five thousand years old. Starhawk, author of the book *Spiral Dance: A Rebirth of the Ancient Religion of the Goddess*, thinks witchcraft had its beginnings close to thirty-five thousand years ago. No matter how old it really is, it wasn't until the third century that any substantial writing on witches and witchcraft can be found.

In 1401, at the instigation of Archbishop Thomas Arundel, England's Parliament established the first law specifically against witchcraft. An accused witch was given the chance to change her beliefs or be burned at the stake. In the years to follow, harsher penalties were attached to the Witchcraft Act.

In 1484, Pope Innocent VII wrote a letter about witches. This was not the first letter written by a pope on how to deal with witches, but it got more attention because, thanks to Gutenberg's invention of movable type, it was possible to print and widely distribute letters. The pope had written the letter because he was concerned that average people and clergy were not taking the threat posed by witches serious enough. Pope Innocent wanted everyone to help find the witches. The situation quickly got out of control as things like the *Witches Hammer*—a witch-hunter's manual— were printed, sparking panic and confusion resulting in the persecution of witches across Europe. Consequently many people were put to death. Today witches refer to this period of time as the Burning Times.

Witches and their beliefs survived the crucible—the severe trial of the inquisition and the Middle Ages. Even though the persecution continued into the seventeenth century, it was much less widespread. In 1604, King James I—you might have seen his name on a translation of the Bible—passed the Witchcraft Act in England.

At the start of the sixteenth century, King Henry VIII provided the death penalty for witches who invoked or conjured an evil spirit; this led to witch hunts like those evident in the Salem trials. The Witchcraft Act of England was again used as a law in Salem, Massachusetts, to prosecute people accused of practicing witchcraft. Maybe you've read

Arthur Miller's play *The Crucible,* which tells the story of the Salem witch trials. The punishment for using witchcraft became hanging. After many years of witch trials, the act was finally repealed in 1736.

In 1736, under George II, a new Witchcraft Act marked a notable reversal in attitude. Now a person who pretended to have the power to call up spirits or foretell the future or cast spells was to be punished as a vagrant or con artist. The punishment now was a fine or imprisonment.

The last person to be convicted under the Witchcraft Act was Helen Duncan in 1944. Authorities feared that Duncan's alleged clairvoyant powers would enable her to betray details of the D-day preparations to the enemy. Duncan ended up spending nine months in prison.

From the eighteenth century onward, those who practiced witchcraft kept their knowledge and powers hidden and stayed out of sight. Because of this, a lot of people thought for decades that witchcraft was dead, yet it was continuing to be passed down to succeeding generations. In the nineteenth century the intellectual community began to consider witchcraft in a different light. The English Parliament repealed the rest of the laws against witchcraft in 1951.

Wicca and Satanism have the same root—denial of the truth—but after that point they really are very different. Wiccans today see their religion, with its origins in ancient occult religions like Druidism, as an acceptable world view all by itself. Wiccans view Satanism as a distortion of the relatively "young" Christian religion.

Wicca is part of the neopagan movement—it attempts to revive the gods and goddesses and nature religions of ancient cultures. Wicca and other neopagan groups draw from many sources, including Gnosticism (salvation from this world through secret, mysterious knowledge), occult writings, Freemasonry (a widespread secret fraternal society), Native American religions, shamanism, spiritism, New Age philosophies, and even science fiction.[15]

The rise in modern witchcraft can be traced to people like Aleister Crowley and Gerald Gardner, who developed new ideas that helped the old image of diabolical witchery fade away, giving birth to a whole new breed of witchcraft.

---

[15]Alan W. Gomes, *Truth and Error: Comparison Charts on Cults and Christianity* (Grand Rapids: Zondervan Publishing House, 1998), 68.

CONTEMPORARY WICCA

In the second half of the twentieth century, a revival of pre-Christian paganism occurred in the United States and Europe. The foundation of this revival was witchcraft, or Wicca (an early Anglo-Saxon word for witchcraft). The Englishman Gerald Gardner, who wrote the novel *High Magic's Aid* and the book *Witchcraft Today*, claimed that he was a witch initiated by a surviving coven, and he imparted much of the alleged lore and rituals of English witches. This all came about after the archaeologist went to Southeast Asia and studied occult practices. He basically combined his Asian occult experiences with Western magical texts and developed a new religion with worship of a mother earth goddess as its focus.[16] Although his claims have been questioned, covens of modern witches sprang up under Gardner's inspiration and spread to the United States in the 1960s. This form of witchcraft consists of feelings for nature, colorful rituals, and a challenge of conventional religion and society.

In 1979, Starhawk wrote *Spiral Dance*, which has become essential reading for most witches. A whole new group of leaders began to emerge—people like Isaac Bonewits, with his practical guidance to living magick, and Scott Cunningham, sharing down-to-earth methods of witchcraft. Wiccan churches started popping up around the country, and online courses became available for those who wanted to learn more serious magick outside of a coven setting.

In 1986, a federal court ruled that Wicca is a legal religion and that the U.S. Constitution protects the practice of it. Some have estimated that in the United States alone there are between one hundred thousand and 1.5 million Wiccans, but the number could be a lot higher since Wicca is a self-styled religion.

Just like there are different denominations for Christians, there are various kinds of witches. Some witches practice rituals in covens, while others work alone and make up their own rituals. Still other witches follow a prescribed set of traditions.

The very nature of Wicca creates an atmosphere for all kinds of

---

[16]George A. Mather and Larry A. Nichols, *Dictionary of Cults, Sects, Religions and the Occult* (Grand Rapids: Zondervan Publishing Company, 1993), 314–315.

traditions to thrive. Here are some of the better-known traditions followed by witches today:

- **Gardnerian.** Founded by Gerald Gardner in Great Britain. It adheres to very structured practices, including ritual nudity and secretive initiations of new members.
- **Celtic.** Distinct feel of Druids with strong focus on the earth, the elements, and tree magick.
- **British Traditional.** Mix of Gardnerian and Celtic traditions. Structured in its practice and not very open to new members.
- **Kitchen Witch.** Focused on the practical side of earth and elemental magick and religion. Popular among city and suburban Wiccans, emphasizing magick in work and domestic environments.
- **Dianic.** Tagged the "feminist" movement of the craft. Mixtures of many traditions with a primary focus on the goddess, in particular Diana. Some have completely left out the male aspect of divinity.
- **Eclectic.** The most modern of the traditions that gives the freedom to mix and match, using whatever suits one best. Most popular form among Wiccans, especially those who practice it alone, because it allows for complete freedom within the framework of the craft.
- **Faerie.** Based on faerie lore, combining natural magick with Celtic and Druid beliefs.
- **Pictish.** A Scottish tradition with very little religious content. Strong connection to nature and the animal, vegetable, and mineral kingdoms. A primary focus on magick.
- **Strega.** Dating back to 1353 in Italy, it is one of the oldest unchanged forms of witchcraft. They worship a god and goddess, meet for full-moon rituals, and celebrate with singing, dancing, and sex. The celebration also consists of a feast of cakes and wine.
- **Teutonic/Nordic.** Rooted in the agricultural and warrior tribes of northern Germany and Scandinavia. The emphasis is on Nordic culture and the worship of the god Odin and the goddess Freya.

MUSIC

As with other religions, music is of great importance in Wicca, both in preparation for and participation in ritual. Magick meditation music or pagan dance music can be ordered online or bought at New Age or metaphysical stores. The group Kiva is a popular band that produces CDs of Wiccan dance music.

Though Wicca has strong appeal for many—not surprisingly in a society that increasingly disdains absolutes—the primary issue is that Wicca promotes a life lived independently of God. The craft is self-centered and encourages you to depend on yourself and the power within you. The God of Creation, who made you and me, says, "For apart from me you can do nothing" (John 15:5). Let's take a look at what God thinks about witchcraft.

WICCA AND CHRISTIANITY

Some involved with the craft believe that Christianity came from Wicca. Nothing could be further from the truth. All you have to do is compare the basic beliefs of each and you will see how different they really are. Since they both can't be right, ultimately your teen must make a choice to decide what they will believe and whom they will follow when it comes to spirituality and faith.

Both the Old and New Testaments make repeated references to the practice of witchcraft and sorcery. In every instance where these practices are mentioned, God condemns them. The Bible condemns all forms of witchcraft, including sorcery, astrology, and magick.

Most Wiccans resent and reject the Bible. They view it as a Christian book with no experiential value and say it is completely out of touch with contemporary society. Yet there is more historical evidence to validate its truth than any other ancient writings. The Bible is God's manual for our lives. For more details on why we can trust the Bible more than any other book ever written, check out the Quick Reference Comparison Guide in Appendix A. I cannot find one book about Wicca that has any kind of support to give it the kind of authority the Bible has.

God is so concerned about witchcraft and sorcery that He very specifically warns us in His Word to stay away from it. In 2 Chronicles we read the story about a man named Manasseh who became a king at the ripe old age of twelve. He did evil in the eyes of the Lord and paid a huge price for his bad choices. Here's what God said about Manasseh's involvement in witchcraft:

> Manasseh even sacrificed his own sons in the fire in the valley of the son of Hinnom. He practiced sorcery, divination, and witchcraft, and he consulted with mediums and psychics. He did much that was evil in the Lord's sight, arousing his anger. (2 Chronicles 33:6)

Just because this story is about a king who lived a few thousand years ago, doesn't mean that God has changed His mind about witchcraft. This warning is just as relevant to us now as it was in previous generations. Provoking God to anger is not a very smart thing to do. Why would God get angry about this kind of practice? Because only He can guide, empower, and direct us, and therefore He wants us to rely only on Him for guidance, strength, and direction. He alone can give us power and life, and He doesn't want to see us deceived and damaged by any imposter.

God uses the Old Testament prophet Micah to warn the Israelites about going to witches for answers about life. "I will destroy your witchcraft and you will no longer cast spells" (Micah 5:12 NIV).

In the New Testament book of Galatians, the apostle Paul warns us to beware of the strong pull of our sinful nature that can cause us to rebel against God and sin.

> The acts of the sinful nature are obvious: sexual immorality, impurity and debauchery, idolatry and witchcraft; hatred, discord, jealousy, fits of rage, selfish ambition, dissensions, factions and envy; drunkenness, orgies, and the like. I warn you, as I did before, that those who live like this will not inherit the kingdom of God. (Galatians 5:19–21 NIV)

What an ugly list of sins witchcraft has been included in! When you carefully consider Paul's warning at the end of this passage regarding the kingdom of God, you realize that God's not kidding. The end of verse 21 is a reminder that someone who persists in such sin is in a dangerous position. It means their destination when they die will not be heaven. God uses even stronger language at the end of the New Testament.

> But cowards who turn away from me, and unbelievers, and the corrupt, and murderers, and the immoral, and those who practice witchcraft, and idol worshipers, and all liars—their doom is in the lake that burns with fire and sulfur. This is the second death. (Revelation 21:8)

We learn from studying the Bible that we only get one shot at life, and then God will hold us accountable for how we have lived.

> It is destined that each person dies only once and after that comes judgment. (Hebrews 9:27)

There is no opportunity to come back over and over again to try to get it right, like Wiccans believe with reincarnation. Heaven and hell are the ultimate realities for everyone's eternal destiny.

Wicca also gives us some confusing information when it comes to the devil. The Bible confirms the reality of Satan and gives us an accurate picture of his true character.

In Ezekiel 28 (NIV) we learn much about Satan. Let's check out a few verses from this chapter in the Old Testament.

- "You were the model of perfection, full of wisdom and perfect in beauty" (v. 12).
- "You were blameless in your ways from the day you were created till wickedness was found in you" (v. 15).
- "Your heart became proud on account of your beauty, and you corrupted your wisdom because of your splendor. So I threw you to the earth; I made a spectacle of you before kings" (v. 17).

Satan was the wisest and most beautiful creature ever made, but he can only do what God allows him to do. Nothing else in all creation could compare to him, yet he made a horrible choice to rebel against God, ultimately plunging all of creation—including you and me—into a life-or-death spiritual war.

Satan's incredible pride led him to rise up against God. He refused to accept the fact that all of his greatness came from God. As his pride grew, he became determined to take over God's kingdom and seize control of His power. Satan, the most beautiful, the most powerful, and the wisest of all created beings, started a war he could never possibly win.

Because of His awesome holiness, God could not tolerate rebellion and evil in His kingdom. God stripped Satan of his position of authority, drove him from heaven, and made a disgrace of him as He threw him to earth. Though this battle between God and Satan started in heaven, we're now caught right in the middle of it here on this planet. And because Satan hates God, he also hates those of us who try to live our lives in a way that pleases the Lord. There's not a chance that the devil's going to let us remain untouched spiritually by his fierce attacks. He's going to throw everything he can in his arsenal of weapons to harass us and keep us from focusing on God, including trying to seduce us into things like Wicca.

God is a Spirit that the Bible represents as our Father. Because He is personal, there is warmth and understanding in our relationship with Him. He is not a department, a machine, or a computer that automatically supplies all our needs. He is a knowing, loving, good Father. He can be approached. God can be spoken to, and He in turn speaks to us. Plus, our relationship with Him is not a one-way street. He doesn't just simply take and accept what we offer. He is a living and reciprocating being whom we meet and know.[17] In Isaiah 9:6 He is called Everlasting Father; Matthew 6:9 refers to Him as our Father in heaven; while in 2 Corinthians 6:18, God says He will be a Father to us.

The Bible also makes it clear that we are not to worship any other gods—including ones that we make ourselves.

> You must worship no other gods, but only the Lord, for he is a God who is passionate about his relationship with you. (Exodus 34:14)

Why would God be jealous? This can be hard to understand, especially because the jealousy we are used to is usually destructive—like a spouse being jealous when his or her mate talks with someone from the opposite sex. But God's jealousy is different—it's appropriate and right. He makes a very strong exclusive demand on us: We must worship only Him as God.

He can make this kind of demand because of His unconditional, sacrificial love for us. He demonstrated this love for us when He allowed Jesus to die for us on the cross (Romans 5:8). In all that I have read about the god and goddess of Wicca, there is absolutely nothing

---

[17]Millard J. Erickson, *Christian Theology*—2nd Edition (Grand Rapids, MI: Baker Books, 1998), 296.

ever mentioned about their sacrificing or dying for anyone, to make a new and eternal life possible.

But let's look at this god and goddess issue from another angle. If we design and make our own gods (deities), they are actually smaller and less powerful than we are. So if we think logically, they are of no real value or help to us. We need a God who is bigger than us; one we can turn to for guidance and power to deal with the difficult issues of life. How big is your God?

The Bible makes it very clear that Jesus is the only way to get to God and ultimately heaven. He is also the key to life on this planet (John 14:6). And did you notice that witches not only talk very little about life after death but they also don't have a solution for the problem of sin and guilt?

As parents, we have a huge responsibility to help our teens choose wisely. It must be done on solid evidence, not on feelings and experiences that can change. To hope to accomplish this, we must listen carefully—give them a chance to fully express themselves, be an example of one who lives by God's truth, and be able to articulate your faith and pray like crazy.

There's too much at stake for this life and eternity to not do all we possibly can to help our teens navigate through the empty deception of Wicca.

CHAPTER 6:

TODAY'S WITCHCRAFT

WITCHCRAFT. THE VERY WORD stirs deep emotions, visions of mysterious rites done in the dark of night, and thoughts of ancient secrets of the occult. Those secrets both lure and frighten you. They hold the promise of power—power to improve your life; to gain the serenity, love, and comfort you have always wanted; and to stop your enemies cold in their tracks.[1]

You may be wondering how your teen could possibly be involved in witchcraft. Although your son or daughter may not be a practicing witch, know that its temptations and influence are everywhere in teen culture. As we saw in the previous chapter, the appeal of Wicca is huge.

Trying to get your arms around today's witchcraft is no easy task—especially due to the fact that it's such a buffet-style, individually practiced religion. There are some common key elements that define not only the beliefs and practices of Wiccans, but the needs practitioners are looking to have met. Power is definitely one of them. Since witchcraft is a very girl-friendly religion, many teen girls get a feeling of empowerment when they practice it. Wicca also presents a very strong position on environmental issues. Many Wiccans have become serious environmentalists in trying to "cause the least harm." It's mystical,

---

[1]Gavin & Yvonne Frost, *The Magic Power of White Witchcraft* (Paramus, NJ: Prentice Hall Press, 1999), 1.

spiritual, and without a doubt experiential—a perfect match for today's teens.

Let's look at some things you need to know about the way witchcraft is practiced today.

THE NEED FOR POWER

Teens are turning to the craft today because this religion appears powerful, glamorous, and definitely not the norm. Teens today are looking for power to change their lives. They view power as something that can make them feel special, overcome challenges in their lives, and sometimes even give them vengeance on someone who has hurt them.

Those involved in Wicca claim to have a depth of power far greater than the average person seems to have. According to the Web site for The Church and School of Wicca, this previously underground religion has much to teach every human about survival and the ethical use of natural intrinsic powers.

Supposedly the creative power of the universe lives in everyone. Those who practice Wicca believe in the "power within" rather than the patriarchal religions' belief in the "power over." They also believe in going *with* nature rather than against it. According to Wiccans, the key is to learn about the powers hidden within them that they've not developed.

Thoughts can turn into action. A witch will think of things he or she would like to change, then transmit those thoughts with the aid of magick power. The thoughts will speed to their target and cause those desired things to become reality. A witch can gain power over others while gaining material things.

Wiccans believe awesome resources are available to the initiated witches who have full knowledge of their powers. This knowledge includes not only learning how to build your power, but also discovering the time of day your power is the strongest.

This power is drawn from several sources, including spirit or the All (god according to their definition), the elements, the ancestors, and the angels. Witches use their own power—power of the mind—to manifest what they need. They believe that over the centuries, humans have become lazy and suppressed many of their instinctive talents, including the power of the mind, and that we access only what we think we need and apparently don't bother to use a huge portion of our mind power. It's from this "unused mind" that abilities are found, such as clairvoyance, telekinesis, and extrasensory perception (ESP). If you're unsure of the definitions, you can find them in the glossary in Appendix C. According to those involved in Wicca, everyone has these abilities, but most people don't use them—sometimes because of fear. However, witches and other enlightened souls strive to strengthen these natural gifts.

Mega-selling Wiccan author Scott Cunningham reminds witches that although personal power is the most potent force at work in folk magick, its practitioners utilize a wide variety of magickal objects borrowed from the spells and rituals of various cultures. Such "tools" are used to lend their own energies, as well as produce the state of consciousness necessary for magickal workings. Folk magicians have always used natural objects as well as expertly crafted tools to strengthen their magical rituals.[2]

The Cone of Power

The cone of power is one of the sources of a Wiccan's power. The three-sided witch's hat, which looks like a triangle, is a symbol that represents the cone of power. According to Silver Ravenwolf in her book *Teen Witch*, witchcraft encompasses three sides (angles) of belief: love, positive creativity, and spirit. Love can soothe the soul, open a door, and make us all one. The witch does his or her best to love all creatures big or small. The bottom of the hat, or foundation of the craft, is love. The second side of the hat is positive creativity. Wiccan belief states that the main purpose of being human falls under the art of creation or how you invest your time. They believe that it doesn't really matter what you do as long as you create in a positive way. Spirit (or the lord and the lady) makes up the third side of the hat. Witches believe that god—in whatever form—exists, is within us and around us, and is willing to help us if we only ask. God is often called the lord and the lady, because witches see god as both masculine and feminine. Other times god is called spirit. Allah, Jesus, and Buddha are all said to

[2]Cunningham, *The Truth About Witchcraft Today*, 27.

be faces of the masculine side of god. Wiccans also give equal importance to the feminine side of God. By putting the three sides of the hat together—love, positive creativity, and spirit—Wiccans create a cone of power from which their magick energy or power comes. Witches believe they can do and make miracles happen for themselves and others through the cone of power.[3]

Crystals and Stones

One of the more recent rediscoveries of ancient folk magick is the use of stones and crystals. Many books have been written about the magic of stones and their ability to improve people's lives. Witches not only appreciate crystals for their intrinsic value and beauty but they also believe stones contain specific energies for magickal use. Some believe that along with herbs, stones may have been the first magickal tools of ancient times.

Clear and colored varieties of quartz crystals are used, including amethyst (purple), carnelian (orange), citrine (yellow), blue quartz, and rose quartz. Witches use many other types of stones besides quartz to gain better health, draw love, attract money, bring peace, and protect against a variety of illnesses. There are more than a hundred stones used in magick that Wiccans believe can be called upon to release or absorb power.

Folk magicians claim to have the ability to work with these "tools" to arouse, program, release, and direct energies within stones. Once they are empowered, these stones are worn, carried, slipped under a mattress, or placed on magickal altars. In the case of crystals, they are stroked on the body and placed around the house to release their beneficial energies.

Herbs

Wiccans view herbs like crystals—possessing specific, distinct energies that can be used in magick. They collect, mix, burn, and brew these seemingly fragrant treasures. A wide variety of herbs—encompassing fruits, trees, flowers, roots, nuts, seeds, seaweeds, ferns, grasses, and all other types of plant materials—are used in folk magick.[4]

---

[3]Ravenwolf, 10.
[4]Cunningham, 30.

Witches believe that the power of herbs can be released in a couple of ways. One can carry them in their pocket, sprinkle them around their house, or burn them as incense, thus releasing the herbs' energies into the air. In the form of oil, they can be blended and rubbed onto the body or added to the bath, or they can be used to anoint crystals or other objects in rituals.

Candles, Colors, and Cords

Wiccans use candles as magickal tools in two ways: as focal points for power and as additional magickal energy that comes from the colors and flames. In some rituals, depending on the magickal goal, candles of specific shapes and sizes are burned. However, most of the time the candle is a simple common shape, and it's the color that's of great importance to the magick ritual.

Psychologists have come to realize that colors can have strong effects on our bodies as well as our subconscious minds. For example, hospital rooms are often painted in soft shades of green or blue to stimulate healing. Prison walls are painted pink so as to calm down violent or disturbed prisoners. Red is used to attract attention as in advertising or with Stop signs and emergency lights. Wiccans also feel that colors have subconscious effects, and they believe candles contain certain energies related to color. When performing rituals, Wiccans carefully select colored candles based on the need. Here's a sample list:

Yellow—intelligence, divination
White—purification, protection, peace
Green—money, fertility, growth, employment
Light Green—improve the weather
Blue—healing, psychism, patience, happiness
Black—negation, absorption of disease and negativity
Red—protection, health, strength, courage, exorcism, passion
Purple—power, healing of severe disease; spirituality and meditation
Dark Purple—calling up the ancient ones
Brown—healing of animals, homes
Dark Brown—invoking earth for benefits
Orange—material gain, to seal a spell, attraction
Pink—love, friendship

The flame of the candle, as well as the objects around it, helps to direct witches' personal power. A witch must be careful to snuff out the candle, not blow it out, otherwise they will blow away the magick.

Wiccans use candles to serve as focal points of natural and personal power in magick rituals. However, one of the most powerful effects of candles is their ability to alter our conscious minds.

Magick with cords is one of the more simple operations that can be used, either alone or with other tools of power. Simple cord magick involves the following:

- choice of cord color
- choice of cord length
- choice of disposable cord, or one they will use again
- choice of divinity

Usually cord magick involves a black, white, or red cord (basic colors of early goddess worship), thirteen inches in length, with the plan of disposing of the cord when the ritual is done.

Cord magick requires the magickal operation of "charging," where each knot is charged with a chant or charm. Disposal depends on the purpose of the spell. Magick is released by drawing a star in the air over the cord while picturing the magick seeping away from the item.[5]

Take a quick inventory. Have you found candles, wax residue, stones, or cords in your teen's bedroom? There's no need to panic—he or she may be experimenting to see if there's anything to what Wiccans believe. Be careful that you don't interrogate or intrude on your teen's privacy, but you need to discuss what you've seen. His or her first response may be, "You wouldn't understand." Ask for more explanation. By the way, you may want to go on a walk rather than trying to talk in his or her room or another spot in the house. You need to get your teen out of their safe environment where he or she can try to escape mentally and emotionally. By going for a walk, you can accomplish a couple of things. You can get your teen in a different environment, and you also remove the typical face-to-face confrontation stance that we often find ourselves in when talking with our kids. You've also

---

created some movement for both of you to let off steam. Above all, make sure you listen very carefully and don't jump to conclusions.

Words, Chats, and Poetry

An important part of Wiccan magick is the breath as well as the sounds and words produced with it. For generations, secret chants and words of power have been passed down from one witch to another. Witches speak words to herbs, stones, and candles during magick rituals designed to program and stir up their energies. They also use magick words to communicate with the power that's inside them. Words alone are not thought to bring about change; rather, they're used to assist in pinpointing a witch's concentration and to allow him or her to perform a particular magickal action. Basically, when a witch speaks to an object (candle, stone, etc.) they're really speaking to their inner self.

Wiccans believe that poetry is one of the most potent forms of ritual speech. It touches the unconscious mind, the mind of dreams, psychism, sleep, and magic. Rhymed words are easier to recall and flow smoothly during rituals.[6] The words used are very important because of their ability to fill the witch with the proper state of mind, allowing him or her to move energy. The words must have personal meaning to the individual witch. Some witches prefer to compose a fresh, simple rhyme that speaks to them rather than use ancient words of power that may be meaningless to them. Words that speak to a witch can be adequate to produce the necessary state of mind and get the power moving.

Once again, take stock of what you may have seen. But before you say or do anything, ask yourself how you obtained your information. Did you violate their space by going through their backpack or a notebook without their permission? Remember to choose your battles. You may have read or seen something that concerns you, but have you bridged the emotional gap sufficiently to dialogue with them about your distress? Remember, if you're going to connect with your teen at such deep levels on significant issues, make sure you cultivate the emotional bond necessary to allow for honesty and openness.

---

[6]Cunningham, 34.

Techniques and Objects

There are many other techniques and objects used by Wiccans in magick rituals. Here's a quick sample:

Knots—used to represent the physical manifestation of a spell. They are used to lend protection to a person or place.

Clay—molded into symbolic shapes.

Mirrors—used to reflect evil and awaken psychic awareness.

Ink—used to create shapes or draw runes.

Sand—poured into specific images (like sand painting).

Water—used for purification.

Food—prepared for specific magickal changes.

Runes—symbols containing within their lines specific energies.

There are lots of rituals and spells. Witches will often make use of two or more of the power tools that we've looked at. Each element is used in a specific way to enable a witch to achieve the necessary results.

DAYS OF POWER

Most religions have holy days throughout the calendar year. Wicca is no different. But to witches, these days aren't just holy, they're days of power. Most Wiccans perform rituals at least twenty-one times a year: thirteen full-moon celebrations—goddess-oriented—and eight solar festivals related to the god. These rites are done by individuals or in covens.

Esbats

An esbat is commonly known as a full-moon ritual. It's a rite that involves the worship of the goddess and a magickal working. Wiccans often gather with their coven on nights with a full moon (every twenty-eight days) for a magickal ritual. They view the moon as a symbol of the goddess, and they also see it as a mystic source of energy—because it reflects light from the hidden sun (light can be equated with power), and because the moon has proven strong effects on the tides and cycles of women and animals. During esbats, Wiccans draw energy from the moon to gain more power in their magickal workings.

Sabbats

Sabbats are decided by the changing of the seasons. They're connected with ancient European planting and harvesting rites, ancient hunting ceremonies plus the solstices and equinoxes. Just like esbats, Sabbat rituals are held at night. Sabbats basically tell the story of a Wiccan legend about the god and goddess. By examining the eight Sabbats of the calendar year, the details of this legend can be found.

There are many versions of the legend, but one of the more popular ones tells of the goddess giving birth to a son, the god, at Yule. Imbolc finds the goddess resting and the god as a growing boy. At Ostara the goddess comes forth fully from her sleep, the god is strong and lusty, and the earth is a splendor of green. At Beltane the god has become a man, and he and the goddess fall in love and unite. At Midsummer the god's strength reaches its zenith, and the goddess is ripe with a mother's power, as her belly swells with child. At Lughnassah the god begins to wane, even as the goddess carries him, growing, within her. At Mabon the goddess reigns and the god prepares to die, a willing sacrifice for the earth and its people. At Samhain the god's death is celebrated, and the world awaits his rebirth from the goddess, once more at Yule.[7]

Following most Sabbats are the sacred meals of cakes and ale. Foods that are representative of each Sabbat are placed on the altar and eaten during the sacred meal. Symbolic crafts may also be linked to the meal. In some instances magick rituals can also take place at this time, but most Wiccans keep the Sabbats as a time for worship.

Esbats and Sabbats can be seen on three levels. First, they are times of religious worship for Wiccans to connect with the god and goddess. Second, Wiccans use these days of power for working their magick to help heal, comfort, and protect their friends and loved ones. They receive help in this process from other deities. Third, these are also times of celebration. Once the worship and work has been completed, it's party time!

As you may have already realized, these days of power contribute to a complex and confusing belief system that can be easily adopted in the "mosaic-style" of teens' thinking today.

---

[7] Morgan, 45–46.

WICCAN MAGICK

Wiccan magick is used to create a magick circle or sphere of power. This is where rituals are performed and tools are purified and charged with energy for use in magickal ceremonies.

One of the most common methods that Wiccan covens use to raise energy is simply called "the dance." Because they see the human body as a storehouse of life-energy, muscular contraction produces readily available power for use in magick. Specific movements are used to build up energy during rituals.

Wiccans recharge themselves in a couple of ways. One of the easiest ways to recharge is to have a good meal, one very high in red meat, along with some red wine to drink. After about three hours the cosmic energy level will have increased. For Wiccans who are vegetarian, power comes from a tree. A witch would simply stand under a large tree, preferably one with smooth bark, in the star position, facing the tree from the western side. Recharging occurs as they stand there for about five minutes with their forehead against the trunk. Another option is to buy or build a large pyramid and sit under it. Sitting still in meditation for fifteen minutes also recharges energy.

WITCHCRAFT (MAGICK) CIRCLE

Wiccan magick is governed by one simple rule: "An ye harm none, do what ye will." Witches would say their magick is performed for positive ends.

Influencing major events requires more power than the living body can contain. This is the time when the witchcraft magick circle is used. Usually this circle is found in a magick witchcraft temple. The temple is a special room or an isolated location outdoors and has been prepared in special magickal ways that include both a physical and a psychic cleansing. On the floor of the room are painted two concentric magick circles, each about one-half-inch wide. The circle defines the ritual area, holds in personal power, and shuts out distracting energies—it creates an atmosphere for the rites. It is constructed with personal power and is usually nine feet in diameter—the number of the goddess—but any size will work.[8] The first circle is used for personal magickal work,

---

[8]Cunningham, *Wicca: A Guide for the Solitary Practitioner,* 57.

while the second circle is used for cosmic work.

In the craft no one may enter a magick circle unless they are properly prepared. This means that a person has either dedicated themselves to spirit, been initiated into the craft by other witches, or is willing to set aside any differences or negativity to work with the witches. To be properly prepared means that before entering the magick circle (the Wiccan church), the mind, body, and spirit have been cleansed of all negativity.[9]

PATHS OF POWER

The bigger the job, the more important it is to choose the right combination of tools. There are lots of tools that witches make use of for raising energy. These ways of raising energy are called paths of power. Some of these include

- meditation
- invocation
- whispering, singing, monotonous chanting, or sing-song chanting
- trance and astral projection
- herbs, oils, and incense
- movement or dancing
- drums or rattles
- ritual

In any given magickal working, a witch may use more than one path of power.

SPELLS

Spells are a big part of a teen's practice of witchcraft, and there are plenty of resources available to them. Books like *The Teen Spell Book: Magick for Young Witches* contain spells like how to heal your past, find your animal totem, find love, meet a famous person, feel rich, make chores easy, make colleges beg for you, and empower yourself. There's also the *Teen Witch Datebook*, a day planner that offers a variety of spells each week.

---

[9]Ravenwolf, 29.

Here's a basic outline of the rules Wiccans follow for good spells:

1. Confirm what is desired.
2. Decide on the motivation.
3. Decide what magick witchcraft method will be used to achieve the goal.
4. Define an alternate target or how excess power will be used.

The primary thing that makes spells work is the emotion invested in them. The right emotion enables a witch to send out an effective pulse of power. In the end, the spells a witch designs him or herself carry more power than any spell found in a book. Those spells and magickal operations that are created will meld creative energy with the forces of the universe.[10]

SIGNS AND SYMBOLS

The Wiccan religion has sacred signs and symbols of power that represent spirit. Here's an example of a few of them. (The symbols can be found in Appendix E.)

The five-pointed star, point up, is known as the pentagram. The pentacle is also a five-pointed star, point up, with a circle around the star. The pentacle stands for earth, air, fire, water, and the spirit of the human, encompassed by the never-ending love (the circle) of spirit. Witches often wear this symbol for protection and an affirmation of their beliefs. Wearing the symbol where everyone can see it isn't necessary; Wiccans believe the symbol carries more power if it's hidden.[11]

In magick a pentagram can be drawn several ways, depending upon the energy needed and the desired goal. The invoking pentagram is generally drawn starting at the top of the star and the banishing pentagram the exact opposite. The invoking pentagram brings energy closer while the banishing one pushes negative energies away.[12]

The sacred spiral represents the dance of divine energy within the

---

[10]Ibid., 134.

[11]Ibid., 31.

[12]*Banishing* is to rid oneself of something or someone—for instance, if a witch wants to rid herself of an enemy, she can stomp out that person's path through the woods, symbolically taking power over his very footsteps. *Invoking* is to call forth energy from the angels, spirit guides, god, goddess, and other spiritual beings.

world of the witch. Drawn clockwise, the sacred spiral brings things closer; drawn counterclockwise, the sacred spiral pushes negative energies away. The spiral also signifies the ancient journey within, because those who do not know themselves can never seek to know what may be outside them.[13]

The equal-armed cross stands for many ideals—the four seasons, the four directions, the four archangels, the four winds, or the four quarters of the magick circle. Drawn from top to bottom and right to left with the right hand, the symbol represents healing energies. Drawn from top to bottom and left to right with the left hand signifies banishing energies. A witch also uses the equal-armed cross to seal a magickal working so that the negative energies cannot reverse the positive efforts of the magickal person.

GOD AND GODDESS

In witchcraft there are many references to the god and goddess. These are additional tools of power available to Wiccans. However, these deities are much different than what you might think. Wiccans are referring to the gods and goddesses that have been created during the course of history by human beings. Prayer and worship to these mascots contain earth-level power that is stored in their images. The gods and goddesses are a major source of power—which is available for witches to supplement the power innate in their living body.[14]

Despite all these tools of power available, Wiccans still maintain that you already possess the ultimate set of tools needed for life-changing power: your body and your mind. While Wiccans use their power to get what they want—heal someone, influence the boss to give you a raise, get the love of their life, or get vengeance on a bully at school—the bottom line is that witches utilize their power to help themselves and improve the quality of their life.

Gavin and Yvonne Frost ask the question, "What's wrong with your life?" They go on to detail the right each person has to a new life.

> No one, least of all kindly Jesus or gentle Buddha, expects or wants you to live in abject misery. So what is wrong with your

---

[13]Ibid., 32.
[14]Frost, 230.

life today that needs fixing today? Name it; then fix it. Consider what spell will be useful, get the equipment you will need, and get out of that chair and do it. We reminded you earlier that the gods help those who help themselves. You must put something into motion. It takes only a small and simple push; but once it is in motion, the result will be unbelievable. Use the following affirmation: Witchcraft power, give me a new life.[15]

All this sounds a bit confusing, doesn't it? Wiccans are trying to find the right combination of tools of power and some form of divinity in order to achieve a desired goal or cope with the problems of life, but when they step back and look at the big picture, they will realize that the power Wicca offers is very self-centered, self-reliant, and limited.

THE SOURCE OF ULTIMATE POWER

Stop and think for a moment. If we lack the power (in ourselves) to begin with—to change our lives, help us cope or whatever the specific need may be—it's pointless to think that we will somehow be able to conjure up some untapped energy reservoir deep inside us. A chant, magick circles, poetry, symbols drawn in the air or worn around the neck, or even colored candles aren't going to help. The problem is that Wiccans continually rely upon energizing themselves (or some other object) with the use of one or more tools of power. But let's go a step further. Wiccans also believe that power can be obtained from rocks, trees, and herbs. Think about it: Why would you look to a rock or herb for energy when you have the power to toss them in the air or grind them up to put in your food?

However, remember that teens are still developing mentally; they're still learning how to use logic and how to amalgamate the bits and pieces of spirituality presented by our postmodern culture. Be sure that when illustrating even the most obvious Wiccan absurdities you don't condescend or ridicule.

In reality, the energy that teens (adults as well) want and need for living must come from a source outside themselves. The source of this power must be bigger than us, and it must be an unlimited supply of

---

[15]Ibid., 227–228.

power or it's of no lasting value. This kind of power can only be found in one place.

It's described in a book and is available to anyone who wants it. This power is limitless and can overcome even the most seemingly insurmountable problems. The source of this power is the living God—the God of the Bible. You may say, "Wait a minute, Steve. Been there, done that." Have you? Have you really taken the time to carefully examine what the Bible teaches, or are you relying on faulty second-hand information? This is too important a subject to just take someone else's opinion. You and your teen may need to look at the evidence for yourselves.

I won't take time here to review the support presented in a later chapter as to how we can know that the Bible is true, accurate, and a supernatural book. Instead, let's look at some characteristics of God described in the Bible regarding His unlimited, everlasting power that's greater than we can ever begin to comprehend. It's the only power that can truly transform someone's life.

Start by looking at God himself. Keep in mind that we're not talking about the human-made god (god and goddess, lord and lady, etc.) or the hundreds of little gods of the Wiccan religion. Nor are we talking about a God who hates women, as Wiccans have falsely stated in their literature. We're also not talking about the "god" within us or the one who dies and is reborn at a certain time each year, as we have seen described in the Wiccan Sabbats.

God is all-powerful, and His infinite power is demonstrated in many ways. He is the one who forms us in our mother's womb (Psalm 139:13–16) and created the heavens (Jeremiah 32:17). Nothing is too hard for Him and He does as He pleases (Psalm 115:3). In ancient times God's power over nature was frequently demonstrated in miracles: everything from the plagues in Egypt to calming a bad storm (Mark 4:35–41) and walking on water (Matthew 14:22–33). God's power is also obvious in his control of the course of history. In Acts 17:26 we read, "From one man he created all the nations throughout the whole earth. He decided beforehand which should rise and fall, and he determined their boundaries." God is the chief Being in the universe, is all-powerful, and is able to do anything that is consistent with His own nature.

One of the most amazing demonstrations of God's power is in

human life and personality. Changing human personality is among the most mind-bending miracles that God performs. It's not easy altering human nature. Yet in respect to power for this life and securing our eternal destiny, Jesus said, "Humanly speaking, it is impossible. But with God everything is possible" (Matthew 19:26).

Still, by far the greatest display of God's power was the resurrection of Jesus Christ from the dead. The Bible speaks of this power in 2 Corinthians 13:4: "Although he died on the cross in weakness, he now lives by the mighty power of God. We, too, are weak, but we live in him and have God's power—the power we use in dealing with you." There is overwhelming historical evidence to prove that Jesus did conquer death. The resurrection is not just a religious myth. Only Christianity has a God who became a man, died on a cross for all people, and was brought back to life again in power after three days. Dead people can't help you, but Jesus can because He's alive! The same power that brought Jesus back from the dead is available to help us deal with the daily issues of life and give us hope for the future.

This power is available 24/7 to those who become followers of Christ—who have a relationship with God. Once we put our faith and trust in Jesus, the Holy Spirit comes to live inside of us and give us power (John 14:12). Keep in mind that this is the same Holy Spirit the Bible teaches gave life to all of creation (Genesis 1:2). Talk about power! God doesn't want us to rely on our own limited strength and abilities. Instead, we're supposed to rely on the power God gives us through the Holy Spirit (Acts 1:8). This power not only helps us face the challenges of life but also enables us to make a difference in our world.

Stop. Before you read any further, I want you to think about something right now. Why would you (or your teen) want to worship and depend on a created object for power, when you can go directly to the all-powerful Creator for help? Read the following verse from the Bible and carefully think about what's being said about you and the search for power.

> Christ is the one through whom God created everything in heaven and earth. He made the things we can see and the things we can't see—kings, kingdoms, rulers, and authorities. Everything has been created through him and for him. He existed before

everything else began, and he holds all creation together. (Colossians 1:16–17)

Now, think about the Wiccan "tools of power" that we looked at earlier. There were stones, crystals, herbs, colors, cones, cords, special days, molded clay symbols, figurines, etc. Does it really make sense to depend on these objects for power when you can get power from the One who made them?

The power that Wicca offers is limited and bogus. Part of the devil's plan is to deceive us and counterfeit all that God is and does. He loves to disguise himself as an angel of light (2 Corinthians 11:14). Because he's a created being (Ezekiel 28:13, 15), his power is limited—in scope and ability. Satan and his demonic servants work at deceiving us by appearing good and alluring. Many unsuspecting teens (and adults) looking for power are following sincerely misled "religious" people into the spiritual deception of Wicca. There are even people in the church—especially teenagers—looking to Wicca for power.

Don't be fooled that getting hold of power through the living God seems so simple—especially compared to what's necessary in Wicca to gain power. And don't get caught up in being able to explain and understand the capacity of God's supernatural power. There's an element of mystery to it; after all, God's power is supernatural. The greatest mistake we could make is to think that we could fully understand it.

How big is your God? Is He bigger than a crystal, herb, or cone of power?

It takes faith to believe in the God of the Bible. But it takes even more faith to try to make sense of Wicca's source for power. If you really want the kind of power that can change your life and help you face the pressures of living in the twenty-first century, why would you want to rely on a created god who dies each year; on hugging a tree to get recharged; or on trying to get power out of a rock? The wise thing to do would be to find the source of unlimited power and plug into it.

When you decide to follow Jesus and establish a personal relationship with Him, you plug into all the power of the universe. The search for power begins and ends with Jesus. Rely on Him to give you the strength to overcome any struggle you may be facing today. Let this promise found in Philippians 4:13 encourage and guide you: "I can do everything through him who gives me strength" (NIV). It comes down to a control issue. If we really want God's power in our lives, we have to surrender control and trust Him. That's not easy, especially in our self-centered world. And that's a big part of the appeal of Wicca— you're in charge, you maintain control. Yet when you realize how powerless you really are, it makes perfect sense to surrender to the living God and rely on Him to give you the power you need. Stop being deceived. Plug into the real source of power.

This is something you as a parent must come to grips with yourself before you can help your teen. The unlimited power that we need and want can only be found in one place—the person of Jesus Christ.

THE GIRL-FRIENDLY RELIGION

There's another key area in today's witchcraft, and it's had a little help from the feminist movement.

Today's witch is young, is beautiful, practices magick, and wields mysterious psychic powers. One such example is WB's *Buffy the Vampire Slayer*.

Buffy's TV show may be off the prime-time schedule, but the influence of this pop culture female witch icon is still being felt. Huge numbers of devout fans still watch reruns on TV or old episodes on DVD and video. Then there are the fans who read and collect the comics or the book series. Buffy is the classic female witch.

When the media pays attention to the Buffy character, they are generally not referring to actress Sarah Michelle Gellar, who plays her, but rather the fictional character Buffy Summers, who has entered the consciousness of thousands of fans—many who have never even seen the show. According to some Wiccans, this kind of attention that pop-goddess icons like Buffy receive is really energy, and an accomplished witch can use this energy in his or her works.

Pop culture is filled with signs of the huge return of goddess-centered art, books, and music. Playwright Ntozake Shange said, "I found god in myself and I loved her fiercely."[16] Some witches would say it's because society is fed up with women being treated like second-class citizens in a male-dominated club. They're usually quick to point

---

[16]Marci McDonald, "Is God a Woman?" (*Maclean's*, April 8, 1996), 46.

to Christianity as the main culprit because it has "taught" that women should be dominated. Wiccans believe that yang energy has been strongly emphasized through centuries of patriarchal influence and technological advancement.[17]

Wiccans would say that the human spirit now thirsts for a new and better balance with the goddess figure, so it's time to reclaim women's spirituality. Women across the continent are searching for new language and rites to reflect the feminine face of God.[18] Many celebrities like Fiona Horne have discovered and embraced this fast-growing spiritual practice in North America. The list of women who practice Wicca includes Tori Amos, Stevie Nicks, Sarah McLachlan, Cybill Shepherd, Roseanne, and Chrissie Hynde.

Witchcraft's public image continues to improve rapidly with teen girls. *Spin* magazine in its "Grrrl Power" issue ranked witchcraft as the top interest among teenage girls.[19] Ad campaigns targeting teen girls have featured actresses as witches, promoting many products including Finesse shampoo and Cover Girl cosmetics. And the appeal to females extended beyond teenagers when *YM Young & Modern* magazine featured two pages on witchcraft with the headline "Witchy Ways!" while *Jane* magazine featured Phyllis Curott, a high-profile witch, as one of their "Gutsiest Women of the Year."[20] Have you seen the bumper sticker "Back off: I'm a goddess" or the button that says, "My Goddess gave birth to your God"?

The Wiccan belief system can be a powerful invitation to teenage girls who feel held back because of gender or who have been victimized sexually or socially by teen guys or older men. Let's face it, being a teen girl today isn't easy, and Wicca can appear to offer you everything needed not only to survive but also to live a satisfying and meaningful life.

---

[17]Wiccans believe the sun and the moon symbolize the concept of the Chinese yin and yang. These are two opposing forces active in the universe. Yin exists in yang, and yang in yin. It's the changing combination of negative and positive, dark and light, cold and hot, which keeps the world spinning and creates Chi—the giving life-force. In all aspects of life, a state of balance should exist between the opposing forces of yin and yang.
[18]Ibid., 48.
[19]Brooks Alexander, *Witchcraft Goes Mainstream* (Eugene, OR: Harvest House, 2004), 49.
[20]Catherine Edwards, "Wicca Casts a Spell on Teenage Girls," *Insight*, October 25, 1999, 25.

FEMININE DIVINITIES

I receive lots of e-mails each month from teens on a variety of subjects, but questions and comments about Wicca happen to be one of the most frequent topics. Many of them talk about the god and the goddess (lord and lady) and the All. While I was writing this chapter, I received an e-mail from a girl who wrote: "I believe in a goddess that embodies the earth and is to me, as my mother." What's the deal with all this girl-friendly stuff?

The feminist movement in the late 1960s had a great deal to do with the resurrection of the craft and goddess religions. According to Michele Morgan—psychic, tarot counselor, and Wiccan—the craft has brought a much-needed counterbalance to the patriarchal systems that have dominated Western culture for years.[21]

According to Wiccan beliefs, way back in the beginning of time—before the earth and anything else—there was the All. The All, a female spirit, was all alone and existed in stillness and silence. She then created her other half—the male spirit. They entwined as one—the two halves of the whole—even though there are two spirits. Together they gave birth to the universe—solar systems, stars, moons, and planets. They also made land and water, plants, animals, and people on the earth.

Wiccans are more into the goddess because she represents the part of the All that is nurturing and compassionate, enabling growth, fertility, and gentleness. They also work with the goddess because of the nurturing fulfillment of her spirituality.

Wiccans believe that the goddess is in everything and is everything. She is not some force that looks down on us from above, but instead dwells in every single thing—in every rock, in every cat, in every drop of rain and inside you.[22] This is also a key principle found in the New Age movement and is called pantheism. This belief allows Wiccans to worship the creation, mother earth (rocks, sun, moon, etc.), rather than the Creator (God).

Much of Wicca is based on feelings and experiences, so when a witch feels like she or he needs more goddess attributes, there are several things that can be done. One possibility is to warm up some cloth-

---

[21]Morgan, 8.
[22]Denise Zimmerman and Katherine A. Gleason, *The Complete Idiot's Guide to Wicca and Witchcraft* (Indianapolis, IN: Alpha Books, 2000), 44.

ing in a dryer with goddess-centered herbs like gardenia blossoms, heather, lemon balm, lemon rind, lily, myrrh, primrose, spearmint, vanilla bean, and violet. By doing this the clothing will be charged with the goddesses' feminine attributes.

Another way to gain goddess attributes is to pick out an herb that's sacred to a specific patroness and use it in perfume or incense in honor of that goddess. Another option linked with this one is anointing candles and light bulbs. Finally, a witch may eat goddess-centered foods like coconut to internalize the lunar goddess, and he or she may wear clothing of a certain color to tap into a particular energy of the universe.[23]

Overall, the goddess energy is supposed to make witches more aware of their intuitive, spiritual nature. She's a reminder to be creative with magick, and she gently motivates personal change. Novelist Susan Swan signed on for a unique spiritual tour—a pilgrimage to an ancient goddess shrine. Swan found herself struck by how powerful the female images of god were. "I do pray to a goddess-like presence. But I don't know whether she's a metaphor for my inner self or whether there's some spiritual force beyond the individual person."[24]

At first glance this sounds fascinating, intriguing—maybe even "warm and fuzzy." But let's step back for another look. In case you haven't noticed, this whole approach is very individualistic—nearly complete freedom of choice at the expense of any meaningful accountability. Besides some confusion, we're dealing a lot with feelings and experiences. There's too much at stake in life—on this planet and for eternity—to not carefully examine the spiritual dimension from more than one perspective.

JESUS, THE BIBLE, AND WOMEN

There are a lot of misconceptions about God's view of women. And there have been in the past and continue to be a lot of abuses of women in the church today by men. Let's try to clear up some of this confusion by going right to the original source—the Bible—and starting at the beginning of human history.

---

[23]Marian Singer, *The Everything Wicca and Witchcraft Book* (Avon, MA: Adams Media Corporation, 2002), 247–248.
[24]McDonald, 49.

The Old Testament book of Genesis says, "So God created people in his own image; God patterned them after himself; male and female he created them" (1:27). Both man and woman were made in God's image. Women have equality with men in creation. They are both at the very high point of creation, and neither sex is higher or devalued.

In God's design women and men have different roles, but both have the same goals. God shapes and equips women and men for diverse tasks, but they all lead to the same ultimate goal—honoring Him. Each role carries exclusive responsibilities and privileges—and there's no room for the belief that one sex is superior to the other.

God has used women in awesome ways throughout history. He chose Deborah to lead the nation of Israel (Judges 4:4); Jael's resourcefulness and brave act rescued a nation (Judges 4:18–21); a woman's wise words and plan of action saved a city (2 Samuel 20:16).

Women had important roles in the early church. Check out what Paul writes in Romans 16:1–2 (NIV). "I commend to you our sister Phoebe, a servant of the church in Cenchrea. I ask you to receive her in the Lord in a way worthy of the saints and to give her any help she may need from you, for she has been a great help to many people, including me." Phoebe was a helper and highly regarded in the church.

There are amazing stories of women who held various leadership positions and were obviously the best people for the job because God chose them. Don't ever forget that God can use anyone to lead His people—male or female, young or old. Don't let the political correctness of our society or prejudices get in the way of leading or following someone. And be very careful of believing spiritual lies and deception that someone is trying to teach you.

Some people have been bothered because there were not any women among the twelve disciples, but it's clear that there were many women among Jesus' followers. Let's look at one example of the attitude that Jesus had toward women. It's in Luke 8:2–3. "Along with some women he had healed and from whom he had cast out evil spirits. Among them were Mary Magdalene, from whom he had cast out seven demons; Joanna, the wife of Chuza, Herod's business manager; Susanna; and many others who were contributing from their own resources to support Jesus and his disciples."

Jesus raised women up from humiliation and servitude to the joy of partnership. Jewish culture forbade women to learn from rabbis, but Jesus treated women with dignity and respect. By allowing these women to travel with Him, Jesus was showing that everyone—man or woman—is equal in God's sight.

WHERE'S DAD?

I met Greg at a summer camp where I was speaking. Walking out of the dining hall after lunch, this football player yelled, "Hey, Russo— can we talk? Ya know that stuff about not knowing who your dad is that you talked about—that's me." Greg started to cry and said, "My dad divorced my mom when he found out she was pregnant. I've never seen or heard from him. It really hurts."

I've lost track of how many teenagers I have spoken with—in person or on talk radio—who've told me a similar story. Then there are the ones who tell me about an abusive father or one who is in jail. The bottom line is that there are a lot of people who either don't have a father or don't have a good relationship with him. So when you try to talk to them about trusting their Father in heaven, their response is "Forget it."

The lack of a positive father-figure in your life can make the goddess worship more appealing, and it can greatly affect your ability to experience the love and guidance of your Father in heaven. I think this is the case for many involved in Wicca. The pain associated with their earthly father has kept them from exploring a relationship with their Father in heaven.

What kind of relationship do/did you have with your father? What kind of father are you to your teen? I was very fortunate with my dad; he was a great father and friend. And even though he is now in heaven, the memories I have are of a man who loved and cared for me. Because I had such a good human father, I didn't have any obstacles to overcome when it came to establishing a relationship with my heavenly Father. But this may not be true for you or your teen. So let's take a look at what the Bible says our heavenly Father is like. But first, try to set aside the mental and emotional baggage you may have with your earthly father. I know it may be difficult, but it'll be worth it. Let's start by reviewing the story of the "Lost Son"—some Bibles call him the

Prodigal Son—in Luke 15:11–24. It's the story of a rebellious, immature young son who left home because he wanted to be free to live life as he pleased.

In this story we see the father watching and waiting for his son to return. He was dealing with a human being with a will of his own. The father in this story was ready to welcome his lost son back home, if he returned. This is a great picture of God, our Father in heaven. His love is constant and patient. God will give us every opportunity to respond, but He won't force us to come to Him. Just like the father in this story, God waits patiently and lovingly for us to come to our senses. Are you a lost son or daughter that needs to come to your senses? Come back to the One who loves you more than you could ever imagine. Let Him set you free to be the person you were created to be. And remember, God has all the power in the universe, and it's available to help put your broken heart and life back together.

But if you're still not convinced, check out these other places in the Bible that talk about your Father in heaven and what He's like. Take time to carefully read these verses and think about what they say. It's powerful stuff.

- Deuteronomy 32:6 talks about the "Father who created you."
- Isaiah 9:6 calls him an "Everlasting Father."
- First John 3:1 talks about how much our "Father loves us, for he allows us to be called his children."

This is not an exhaustive list of the characteristics of our heavenly Father, but it's a great place to start. Once again, until you as a parent have wrestled with this issue, you can't help your teen son or daughter. And in this day of single-parent families, it's even more important.

Let's look at something Wiccans feel is very important.

TEENS AND THE ENVIRONMENT

Wiccans view the earth as a living goddess who blesses us and must be nurtured and cared for in return. They honor and work with the cycles of nature and the seasons rather than trying to dominate their environment. The Wheel of the Year—the Wiccan sacred calendar—is marked by eight festivals that celebrate the eternal cycle of life, as witnessed in nature by the changing of the seasons and the natural cycles of birth, maturation, death, and resurrection.[25] Ecological issues are of great importance to Wiccans, and consequently they've developed a reputation for being sensitive to and wanting to protect the environment.

Many teen Wiccans have become serious environmentalists in trying to "cause the least harm." The central principle in Wicca is the Rede, and in its somewhat archaic language it says: "An ye harm none, do what ye will." So the question most Wiccans ask a lot—especially when doing magick—is "How can I do the least harm?" They believe that we are all one—with spirit, with people, with plants, with animals, and with the elements.[26] Wiccans believe strongly in the integrity and freedom of the animal kingdom. Some witches are vegetarians, but those who do eat meat give thanks to the animal that gave its life in order for others to eat.[27]

Wiccans recycle trash, and some compost their food scraps or give them to animals to eat. Others buy only organic produce—vegetables and fruit grown in such a way as to cause the least harm to the earth and its inhabitants. If a witch cuts a branch from a tree, the next action is to give something back to the tree—some compost or leaf mold to help nourish its continued growth. When a witch harvests a plant, he or she tries to do it in such a way that is least harmful to the plant. Because Wicca is a nature religion, Wiccans see the goddess in everything—and they honor the goddess by living in harmony with nature.[28]

Wicca allows one to develop a constant, interactive relationship with spirit in as simple a way as seeing the moon come up through the trees and feeling a breathless kinship to her beauty and power, to receiving specific assistance for anything from finding a parking space to mending a relationship.[29] Wiccans believe that we (humans) have an undividable relationship with the earth.

The problem here is with their motivation—to honor mother earth as the living goddess, and to nurture and worship her is by putting people, plants, animals, and spirit/god all at the same level.

[25]Morgan, 8.
[26]Ravenwolf, 18.
[27]Zimmerman and Gleason, 14.
[28]Ibid., 14–15.
[29]Morgan, 32.

ALL ONE AND ALL EQUAL

In the introduction to the *Teen Witch Datebook,* Wiccan author and elder Raymond Buckland writes, "I also envy you (teens) because you are embarking on an exciting journey with incredible rewards. This is a religion and a practice of nature, showing and demonstrating that we are all one and all equal—humans, animals, plants, trees; everything animate and inanimate is closely related."[30] This is beginning to sound a lot like the New Age movement that was so popular in the late '80s and early '90s. Is this really an exciting journey, or a dangerous one of spiritual deception?

Time magazine calls the New Age "a combination of spirituality and superstition, fad and force, about which the only thing certain is that it is not new." Really, the New Age is nothing but ancient Hinduism and occultism repackaged. Leaders within the movement say it's amazing what you can get people to do when you take away the Hindu and occultic terminology and use language for the twenty-first century.[31]

The New Age can be defined as the growing penetration of Eastern and occultic mysticism into Western culture. The term *New Age* refers to the Aquarian Age, which some New-Agers believe is dawning, bringing with it an era of enlightenment, peace, prosperity, and perfection. Spiritual deception! It's just another tool to lure us away from God's truth.

Check out the following two principles found in the New Age movement and see if they don't sound a lot like Wiccan beliefs.

1. All Is One. One Is All. (Monism)

According to New-Agers, every little particle in the universe and every piece of matter everywhere is interconnected. Everything swims in this huge cosmic interconnected ocean. There is no difference between rocks, trees, humans, animals, and God. We are all the same. Allegedly, the reason we have problems in our world today is not because of evil, but ignorance. We are ignorant of the fact that we are all interconnected.

---

[30]Raymond Buckland, *Teen Witch Datebook* (St. Paul: Llewellyn Worldwide, 2002), 4.
[31]*Time* magazine, December 7, 1987, 62.

2. God Is Everything. Everything Is God. (Pantheism)

New-Agers say that everything in creation is part of God—trees, animals, people, etc. Everything has a divine (God-like) nature. It is part of God. The idea of a personal god needs to be abandoned. You don't need a savior because you are *part* of God. If a god (he or she) does exist at all, "it" really just started a big bang many years ago and is now just an impersonal force floating around in the cosmos somewhere.

Sound familiar? Of course, because these are things that Wiccans also believe. These kinds of principles allow Wiccans to worship the creation, mother earth (rocks, sun, moon, etc.), rather than the Creator (God).

Being responsible when it comes to the environment is a value made clear in God's Word, but the Wiccan perspective of worshiping the earth is a reversal of biblical teaching. Let's establish a healthy and God-centered view of caring for the environment, in contrast to the cultural assumption that Christianity promotes the greedy exploitation of creation. It's an important lesson to pass on to the next generation.

God not only created everything and is separate from it, He holds it all together as well. "In the beginning God created the heavens and the earth" (Genesis 1:1). "For by him all things were created: things in heaven and on earth, visible and invisible, whether thrones or powers or rulers or authorities; all things were created by him and for him. He is before all things, and in him all things hold together" (Colossians 1:16–17 NIV).

Think about it: If God were just a part of creation, He wouldn't be much of a god. He couldn't help us, protect us, and provide for us. And who would hold everything together and keep it from disintegrating into chaos? The balance in nature is a result of God's design. "But God made the earth by his power, and he preserves it by his wisdom. He has stretched out the heavens by his understanding" (Jeremiah 10:12).

As people, we are able to think logically, love, forgive, and even set up laws to live by. Most important, we are able to establish a personal relationship with our Creator. And there's no doubt that God loves all He created (Psalm 65, 104, 145, 147, 148). But the Bible is very clear that God values people above everything else in creation. Check out the words of Jesus in Matthew 6:26. "Look at the birds. They don't need to plant or harvest or put food in barns because your heavenly

Father feeds them. And you are far more valuable to him than they are." You should also check out verses 25, 27–34 of the same chapter. We're not equal with creation nor are we equal with God. The Bible also tells us that we (humans) are separated from God because of our sin (Romans 3:23).

However, because we live in the natural world, we are responsible for how we manage it. The Bible teaches that we were made for relationships—with God, with other people, and with creation—which directly contradicts what Wicca teaches. God is not an impersonal force or an "it." He is alive and is our Lord and Savior. The Bible is filled with His characteristics, and they tell us what kind of a great and awesome God He really is (Deuteronomy 6:4; Ephesians 1:3).

It's interesting to realize that creation and our fate are closely tied together. And both will experience restoration and a bringing together of God with His creation.

We don't have to be bummed out or paranoid, because God has promised to make a new earth and heaven. We also have the hope of being completely transformed by God's power. We won't be reincarnated or recycled. There will be no more sickness, cancer, or AIDS because we will have new bodies. God already started this process spiritually when Jesus died on the cross to pay the penalty for our sin.

God has commissioned all of us—adults and teens—to use our creative abilities to make planet Earth a better place to live. As we serve God, we should do everything that we can to manage all of creation in the best way possible and equip the next generation to do the same.

COMPLEX AND CONFUSING

If after reading this chapter you are still having trouble getting your arms around today's witchcraft, you are not alone. The variety of felt needs and issues we looked at are important and need to be dealt with in a proper, biblically based way. This is the main objective that teens need to grasp: God does have a better way to deal with these issues. Parents face not only a huge challenge but also have a great opportunity to help their teens unpack Wiccan beliefs and dialogue together about them. Ultimately, you need to bring them to a place in your discussion where you can make a comparison between these beliefs and what the Bible teaches. Of course, this takes time and patience.

Along with Wicca's appeal comes a certain amount of complexity and confusion. That's just part of the price tag of a self-styled religion. Hopefully you now have a better idea of how and why teens—perhaps including your own—might be attracted to and plugging into Wicca. The war on Wicca is winnable, but you need to have a strategy. And in the remaining chapters of this book I hope to provide that for you.

CHAPTER 7:

HAVE YOU LOST YOUR IDENTITY?

THE 1990s GENERATED a new variety of crooks called identity thieves. Their stock in trade? Your everyday transactions, which generally reveal bits of your personal information: your name, address, phone numbers, bank and credit card account numbers, your income, or your Social Security number. An identity thief obtains some piece of your sensitive information and uses it without your knowledge or permission to commit fraud or theft.

Identity theft is a serious crime. People whose identities have been stolen can spend months or years—as well as a considerable amount of their hard-earned money—cleaning up the mess thieves have made of their good name and credit record. In the meantime, victims may lose job opportunities, be refused loans, education, housing, or cars, or in extreme cases get arrested for crimes they didn't even commit.

What about you—have you had your identity stolen? It can be quite a hassle. But there's another kind of identity theft that takes place, and it can actually be much more damaging to your life—your spiritual one. This is the essential character of who you are at your very core. It's about your security, significance, and acceptance—those things that make up your true identity.

Have you lost it? Has it been stolen by your spiritual adversary, the devil? This is a huge problem among both teens and adults today. I'm convinced the reason so many teens struggle with their identity is because their parents are still struggling with who they are.

Let's face it, we all want to belong. We want people to like us. We want to feel significant. This was a big struggle for me as a teenager. I had a horrible self-image—I hated myself. I would stand at my locker and curse God for making me look the way I did. Besides being tall and skinny—my nickname was "Sticks" not just because I played drums, but also because my legs were so skinny—I had dark, curly hair. It was your basic 'Fro. I wanted straight blond hair. Unfortunately, my parents wouldn't let me bleach my hair so I tried everything I could think of to straighten it. Hair gel didn't work, and blow-drying it only made it worse. Then I had two fangs sticking practically straight out of my mouth. When I laughed or smiled, I covered my mouth with my hand because I was so embarrassed.

The worst thing of all was my mother's fault. I'm convinced my mom gave birth to a five-pound nose and my body grew off it!

I was desperate for relationships. I wanted to fit in and feel like I belonged. But I didn't think anyone could like me unless I was sitting behind a set of drums. The drums became my life, my security, my significance, my vehicle for acceptance.

Sound familiar? Teens and adults place a huge value on belonging to a particular "tribe" or group. This is their circle of closest friends— kind of like a family. It's a struggle to define yourself and be set apart to belong to a group of like-minded peers. For teens, things like clothing styles, tattoos, and body piercing are symbols of core values that associate them with a particular subculture. For adults it can be things like cars, houses, country-club memberships, and job positions.

And for some, no matter what you do or possess, you just don't seem to fit in, and that hurts. Everyone has been wounded by others, but it's especially damaging when it comes at the hands of those who say they're Christians. Take what happened to shock-rocker Marilyn Manson, for example.

Manson, born Brian Warner, was raised in the Episcopal Church and went to a nondenominational Christian school. But he never really fit in and got picked on a lot for being different. Now he says he identifies with Satan. "So that was the point where I started to seek out other interpretations of God. And initially, when you rebel, you go for the obvious choices—heavy metal, Satanism. To me, Satan ultimately represents rebellion. Lucifer was the angel that was kicked out of heaven because he wanted to be God. To me, what greater character to identify with?"[1]

If Christians are seen as being elite, judgmental, two-faced, and phony, it's easy to seek an alternative religion that won't demand that you conform to an illogical external standard of dress or appearance. Wicca provides that sense of acceptance for teens.

But the question is: By what and by whom? To start with, many teens who practice Wicca are solitaries—individuals who prefer to practice the craft on their own, working out their rituals privately and pacing their spiritual journey as they see fit.[2] Then there's the nebulous All and the god and goddess or lord and lady. Add to this the deities that Wiccans get to design and create. Wicca can appear to be an easy place to find belonging and a sense of identity.

Do you feel like you belong and really know who you are? This is another area of spiritual deception that even as adults we sometimes fail to recognize. If the devil can keep us confused about our true identity, he'll keep us frustrated, lacking confidence, and we will not experience a satisfying and fulfilling life. And if we are struggling in this area, we won't be of much help to our kids.

Knowing who you are—having a solid identity—is the key to a meaningful life. When we come to grips with who we are, our whole perspective on life dramatically changes. But many people don't know how to find their identity (it takes more than a magical incantation or spell!), and when they do, they often don't want to believe it. They're afraid they might have to become someone they don't really want to be.

Your identity—security, significance, and acceptance—can only be found in a personal relationship with God through His Son, Jesus. Knowing who you are in Christ will dramatically impact every dimension of your life.

---

[1] *www.beliefnet.com.*
[2] Morgan, 24.

HOW NOT TO FIND OUT WHO YOU ARE

Telling me your name, where you live or work, your stock-market portfolio, or what you like to do for recreation are all things about you. But even with all that information, you still haven't told me who you really are.

Who we are is not determined by what we do, where we live, work, or even the stuff we possess.

I was in London, England, leading a saturation evangelism team as part of a large citywide outreach. We knocked on the door of one particular flat and were greeted by a well-dressed elderly lady. She invited us in and asked if we would like a cup of tea. She showed us around her beautifully decorated home that contained some fantastic paintings and antiques. I inquired about her husband, only to find out that he had passed away about nine months prior. She said, "My husband was a good man and he left me very well taken care of financially. I live very comfortably and have plenty of money, but something's missing. Ever since he died I struggle with who I am and why I'm here."

I had the chance to tell her about who was missing in her life— Jesus. And that He was the One who could make sense out of her identity issues. I wish I could tell you that she placed her faith and trust in Christ right then and there—she did not. She wanted time to think it over, but she did promise to attend one of our larger meetings later that week in the stadium.

When I was in high school I did well in academics and sports, but my passion was music. It was my life. So when I went to my high school class reunion, people thought I was still doing the music gig. They would come up and say, "Hey, Russo. Who are you playing with and recording with now?" When I responded that I was now in full-time ministry, they didn't know what to say. It was almost as if I'd told them I had some strange tropical disease that was highly contagious. They politely said "bye" and walked away. All through high school everybody had my identity wrapped up in the drums. And so did I.

The confusion over identity can work the opposite way as well. If you can't perform or you don't have the status or possessions society says you need, you may start thinking of yourself as worthless. You may see yourself as a failure because you didn't get the big promotion, or your vacation wasn't as exotic as your neighbors'. Or maybe you've heard for a long time from your parents, co-workers, or friends that you'll never succeed in anything.

I took a speech/communication class my freshman year of college. One day after class the professor asked to speak with me privately. "Mr. Russo, there's one thing I want to encourage you never to consider as a profession—public speaking," she said. "You're awful. You mumble and can't speak clearly. Your mannerisms are bad. You just don't have what it takes." That's strange, isn't it? Today I speak to audiences all over the world: face-to-face and on the radio and TV! I'd like to find that professor today and let her see what God can do in a person's life.

Have you discovered your true identity? Do you really know who you are? Who you are is determined by much more than what you have, what you do, and what you achieve. Just ask Keith Wegemen.

DISCOVERING WHO YOU ARE

As far back as he could remember, Keith's main goal in life was to make the Olympic ski team. Finally, in 1952, he was chosen for the Olympics. After months of practice, Keith headed to Europe for the games. The day finally came when he was to experience the greatest thrill of his life. There he stood at the top of the world's highest ski jump at Oberstdorf, Germany.

For a frozen moment in time, he paused all alone, 650 feet above the outrun of the jump. The eighty thousand people below him seemed no bigger than ants. Then the signal was given and the crowd was silent as he plummeted down at over eighty miles per hour. His senses couldn't keep up with the scream of the wind and the blur of trees, snow, and sky. Then suddenly he was hanging motionless over the white hill below. After what seemed like an eternity, Keith landed sixteen feet beyond the four-hundred-foot mark, the longest jump an American skier had ever made up to that time.

Two weeks later Keith was on a plane headed back to New York. The Olympics were over. Now what? As the engines droned on endlessly, somewhere over the Atlantic the questions hit him: *What, then, does last? What's important in the long run? What's the answer?* He was twenty-three years old and had never thought about these questions before. Once he arrived home, he couldn't seem to find any thrills that would last—they all wore thin quickly, even the celebrity status he now had with all the endorsements and appearances.

Sometime later he was visiting his brother and some friends in Southern California. They invited him to attend a young adults' conference in the San Bernardino Mountains. He attended a few of the meetings but spent most of his time swimming, climbing, and hiking. Still, Keith decided he'd better make an appearance at the closing meeting. The auditorium was hot and he didn't really listen too much, until the speaker was toward the end of his message and started talking about pleasures in this life that don't last. Keith sat straight up in his chair when he heard the speaker say, "What, then, does last? What's important in the long run? What's the answer?" He couldn't believe his ears. Those were the exact same questions he asked while flying over the Atlantic.

"Do you want to know the answer?" the speaker continued. Keith bent forward in his chair and heard, "Try Jesus." He jumped up and ran outside toward the safety of the mountain. After an hour, he finally stopped, sat down on a slope, and let the words he'd been running from catch up to him. He had known about Jesus as an idea or principle, but now he would know Him as a person. Keith's life would never be the same. Now he had a different kind of thrill to live for—one that wouldn't wear thin.

Keith found out what everyone on this planet needs to know: You become complete as a person and have a life of meaning and purpose when you find your identity in Jesus. This happens when we surrender our lives and put our faith and trust in Him—the living God. This is something that Wicca can't offer.

It's only in Jesus that we find out who we really are. And that's what finally happened to Keith. He was confronted with the truth and came to love the One who knew him better than anyone else—even better than he knew himself. Keith found out about the One who put him together, piece by piece, molecule by molecule, in his mother's womb. In Jesus his true identity was found. And this knowledge totally transformed Keith Wegemen's life.

How about you? Have you come to grips with who you are in Jesus? Do you realize that He loves you just the way you are? You're somebody special in His eyes. Nothing in witchcraft even comes close to this, yet teens and adults are caught in this trap of the mystical emptiness of spells, incantations, and self-made deities, desperately trying to figure out who they are.

God created you as a unique individual. Billions of people have been born and walked the face of this planet, yet there has never been any two who are exactly alike—not even identical twins. Here's something that describes this fact perfectly. It's called *I'm Special* from that famous author, Anonymous. After you read it, take some time to let the message really soak in.

I'm Special

I'm special. In all the world there's nobody like me. Since the beginning of time, there has never been another person like me. Nobody has my smile. Nobody has my eyes, my nose, my hair, my hands, my voice. I'm special.

No one can be found who has my handwriting. Nobody anywhere has my tastes—for food or music or art. No one sees things just as I do. In all of time there's been no one who laughs like me, no one who cries like me. And what makes me laugh and cry will never provoke identical laughter and tears from anybody else, ever. No one reacts to any situation just as I would react. I'm special.

I'm the only one in all of creation who has my set of abilities. Oh, there will always be somebody who is better at one of the things I'm good at, but no one in the universe can reach my combination of talents, ideas, abilities, and feelings. Like a room full of musical instruments, some may excel alone, but none can match the symphony sound when all are played together. I'm a symphony.

Through all of eternity no one will ever look, talk, walk, think, or do like me. I'm special. I'm rare.

And in all rarity there is great value. Because of my great rare value, I need not attempt to imitate others. I will accept—yes, celebrate—my differences. I'm special.

And I'm beginning to realize it's no accident that I'm special. I'm beginning to see that God made me special for a very special purpose.

He must have a job for me that no one else can do as well as me. Out of all the billions of applicants, only one is qualified, only one has the right combination of what it takes.

That one is me. Because . . . I'm special.

This is just the start. Now that you're beginning to realize how special you really are, let's take a closer look at how to begin developing your true identity.

YOUR TRUE IDENTITY

In the Bible we learn that when you establish a relationship with Jesus Christ, you have a new life. "What this means is that those who become Christians become new persons. They are not the same anymore, for the old life is gone. A new life has begun!" (2 Corinthians 5:17). When you put your faith and trust in Jesus, you become a brand-new person on the inside, a person who didn't exist before. Ephesians 5:8 puts it this way: "For you were once darkness, but now you are light in the Lord. Live as children of light" (NIV). There isn't anything more dramatically different than darkness and light. This is how different your life will be once you recognize who you are in Jesus Christ.

This concept is often misunderstood today, so let's clear up some of the confusion. To begin with, did you know that there are two births you can have in life? A physical one and a spiritual one. When you are born physically, the result is physical life. When you are re-born spiritually, you receive eternal life.

When you are born spiritually, it opens up all the other dimensions of your life—social, emotional, physical, intellectual—enabling you to become the person God designed you to be. All of a sudden life starts to make sense. A new life in Christ gives you a brand-new identity. Becoming a Christian is not just something you add to your life—it's something that becomes your life. You're not rehabilitated or reformed. You may look the same on the outside, but you're a radically different person on the inside.

As a brand-new person, God also gives you a new heart. You have been completely forgiven of all your sin and given a new start at life. That means you can stop living under the cloud of guilt about your past. Start experiencing life as the person God designed you to be. The penalty for your sin has been paid in full by Jesus' dying on the cross.

And you've been given an awesome new power to overcome the difficulties in life as well. The power you now have available to you is the same power that brought Jesus back to life from the grave on the very first Easter Sunday. It's called resurrection power, and it's available to help with all the difficult issues and pain in your life. This power never runs out, and you can only get it from the living God of the Bible.

Wicca offers limited power that basically "comes from within you." With Christ you are connected to unlimited power from the all-knowing, living God.

Life isn't always easy for teens or adults in today's world. Broken families, money problems, unrealistic expectations, abuse, and stress can get you down. Things get even more complicated when you add the spiritual battle that is raging in our lives. Don't get too overwhelmed. Learn to trust God. Take it one step at a time. When you learn to rely on Him with the small things, it will be easier when dealing with the big stuff. And remember, your kids are watching you to see how you handle the difficult issues of life. When they look at you, what do they see?

There's a promise found in Jeremiah 29:11. "'For I know the plans I have for you,' says the Lord. 'They are plans for good and not for disaster, to give you a future and a hope.'" God wants you to get the most out of life. When you have secured your eternal destiny and identity through Christ, it should affect the quality of life you live here on earth. There will always be problems, stress, and struggles, but the way you respond is going to be much different because now you have all the resources of the living God giving you power to enable you to face the challenges head-on.

It's extremely important to recognize that you're not the same person you once were after you have established a relationship with Jesus. If you're thinking to yourself, *Steve, I accepted Jesus and I'm still struggling with my identity and my self-image,* then you're still being deceived. The devil has distorted the truth about your identity. Stop listening to his lies and start living God's truth. Satan would like you to believe that nothing's really changed. But God no longer sees us as we once were.

God changes us so completely in Christ that even He looks at us differently. "For we are God's masterpiece. He has created us anew in Christ Jesus, so we can do the good things he planned for us long ago"

(Ephesians 2:10). Since God considers us His masterpieces, we shouldn't treat ourselves or others with disrespect.

Meaning and purpose in life that lasts cannot be found outside of Jesus. Stop wandering down the empty, experiential, psychic path of Wicca. If you have a relationship with God through Jesus, you are a child of God. Live in an appropriate way. Check this out: "But to all who believed him and accepted him, he gave the right to become children of God" (John 1:12). Since our Father in heaven is the Lord of lords and the King of kings, what does that make us? Children of the King. Talk about significant! Are you living like the royalty you truly are?

Paul challenges us to live lives worthy of who we are: "Therefore I, a prisoner for serving the Lord, beg you to lead a life worthy of your calling, for you have been called by God" (Ephesians 4:1). What happens when Prince Charles of England goes anywhere? How is he treated? People literally roll out the red carpet for him. Heads of State and bands greet him. People take extra special care of him. He even has bodyguards for protection. Why? Because he is royalty and the future king of England.

But if you are a follower of Jesus, you have a much greater heritage and inheritance than even Prince Charles. You are a child of the King of the heavens, and you will rule forever with the Lord of all creation.

HOW GOD DESCRIBES WHO WE ARE

The Bible is filled with incredible descriptions of our identity in Jesus Christ. Let's take a look at some of the verses that can help us get an even better idea of who we really are.

In 1 Corinthians 6:19–20 we read: "Don't you know that your body is the temple of the Holy Spirit, who lives in you and was given to you by God? You do not belong to yourself, for God bought you with a high price. So you must honor God with your body." What was the cost of buying your freedom from the powers of darkness? It was the very life of God's only Son, Jesus. God paid the highest price possible so your relationship with Him could be restored and your true identity secured. Isn't it amazing how valuable you are to God and how much He loves you?

Knowing that we were bought with such a tremendous price should cause us to be more careful in the way we live our lives. You don't have to "loan yourself out" in a bad relationship, sell out your values to climb the corporate ladder, or abuse drugs and alcohol to feel worth something or escape the pain. There's no reason to compromise any longer to get someone to love you. God will provide for all your needs. You were bought with the ultimate price, so live like it and don't settle for anything less.

Colossians 1:13 describes the security that is part of our identity: "For he has rescued us from the one who rules in the kingdom of darkness, and he has brought us into the Kingdom of his dear Son. God has purchased our freedom with his blood and has forgiven all our sins." Before we surrendered our lives to Christ, you and I were hostages of the devil to do his will (2 Timothy 2:26). We were prisoners, but God set us free! And Jesus promises that once we are His, no one can take us from Him (John 10:28).

Do you remember the response of some of the Iraqi citizens after the Coalition forces, as part of Operation Iraqi Freedom, had liberated their city? There was dancing in the streets, people hugging each other, and in some cases Iraqi men even wanted to kiss the soldiers for setting them free! The celebrations were fantastic. It seemed like a lot of people in the world partied.

But did you know that there is an even greater celebration for those who are set free from Satan's prison? Check out the words of Jesus in Luke 15:7: "In the same way, heaven will be happier over one lost sinner who returns to God than over ninety-nine others who are righteous and haven't strayed away!" When someone accepts Jesus Christ, it's party time in heaven! Spiritual freedom through Jesus is secure and lasts forever.

Next time you're feeling insecure because co-workers have rejected you or things are tough with your spouse or kids, stop and think about your security in Christ. Let this knowledge about your true identity influence your behavior. There's no need to fear anyone or anything that life may throw at you. "For God has not given us a spirit of fear and timidity, but of power, love, and self-discipline" (2 Timothy 1:7). Having a relationship with Jesus can truly make a difference in the way you live.

Isn't it amazing how many dimensions of life our identity (or lack of it) affects? And imagine what not having a clear grasp of their true identity is doing to your teen.

With Jesus we have everything we'll ever need to make life worth living. That's not to say we don't want other relationships or a fulfilling career, but without knowing who we are in Christ, everything else is meaningless. "How we praise God, the Father of our Lord Jesus Christ, who has blessed us with every spiritual blessing in the heavenly realms because we belong to Christ" (Ephesians 1:3). Our minds can't even begin to comprehend what God has blessed us with or has planned for us to experience (1 Corinthians 2:9). Don't miss what you can experience through Jesus by continuing to search for something more in the deception and emptiness of Wicca or some other religion.

KNOWING WHO WE ARE AFFECTS HOW WE ACT

If we could really grasp what our identity in Christ means as adults in our day-to-day experiences, I'm convinced we'd see some of the problems that plague us shrink and maybe even disappear altogether. It would also revolutionize our families.

I could fill pages with youth culture issues that have their roots in the problem of identity. We could talk about teens struggling with eating disorders, suicidal tendencies, or kids who cut themselves, and we'd keep coming back to the fact that knowing who we are affects how we act. I don't want to sound overly simplistic, but so many teen problems today could be solved by helping them find their true identity in Christ and letting that influence the way they live.

Some of the most frequent questions teens ask me are, "Why am I here?" "Give me a reason to get up in the morning," "How can I make a difference with my life?" But many adults ask the same questions. All of these and more can be answered in one word—*Jesus*. Whether you want to admit it or not, Satan will try to deceive you into not believing this awesome truth. He started doing this back in the beginning of human history with the first man and woman—Adam and Eve—and he hasn't changed his strategy since. Deception is his greatest weapon, especially when it comes to our identity. Satan knows all too well that the truth about who you are is the thing that will set you free. Jesus said, "I am the way and the truth and the life" (John 14:6). Lasting security, acceptance, and significance will only be found in Christ.

Our teens are not going to find their identity—security, significance, and acceptance—in a force called the All or by worshiping the earth. And you'll never find your security, significance, and acceptance in chasing the illusive American dream.

The only place you and your teen are going to find your real identities is in a vital, intimate relationship with Jesus Christ. This happens by surrendering your heart and life to Him, and saying, "Jesus, I want you to invade my humanity and help me to become the person I was designed to be so I can experience a rich and satisfying life."

You find yourself through surrendering your life—an act of your will—to the living God of the Bible. When you find yourself in Him, your life will never be the same—on this planet or in life after death.

CHAPTER 8:

RELIGION ANY WAY YOU WANT IT

WE LIVE IN A CULTURE where truth is relative and it's trendy to custom-design your own belief system and morality. Everyone seems to be doing it. I was online and checked out an ongoing forum chat about "Christian witchcraft." Here's some of the discussion that was taking place:

- "I figure since a lot of pagans use different gods and goddesses, then why not just use 'God' or JC? Maybe incorporate some saints? Or even angels? I haven't used them in any of my magickal works yet, but I plan to. There are some great angel spells out there like a guardian angel spell which is seemingly really easy." GT

- "I look at it that God doesn't care what you believe, just that you do and that belief kind of revolves around what are, for me at least, universal truths of decent behavior. You don't lie to each other. You don't steal from each other. You respect your elders— even if you don't like them, because everyone has something to teach even if it's only, 'Don't do this.' You don't kill people just to kill them. You celebrate life and the beauty it entails and try to learn to be appreciative that you have been given the opportunity to experience it, regardless of how many times you may have." DH

- "Did you notice that in the bible it says do not have any other gods before me, it doesn't say that there isn't any—just don't have them before him or her or it. Therefore, I am under the assumption that there are many gods, deities/saints, and other higher beings or wherever they are. Just don't worship them over him, meaning don't pick them over me. Personally when I started to practice magick I started with witchcraft. Loved it but couldn't get around all of the gods and goddesses that were being called to aid them in their work or help them, etc. That is my Christian side coming out. So I was conflicted for a while, thinking what do I do, how do I get around this obstacle and still practice magick. I didn't like calling on the divine, even Christian divinity, saints, etc. I felt and still feel now that all they are, divine beings, gods servants. All they do is provide much concentrated energy when called upon by a mage or witch. Of course it is more powerful because it's more concentrated and coming from a divine being, but energy is all around us, we can raise enough to get the same results they do. It might take longer and take experience and practice, but we can all do it. So I started to get into energy magic. Raising energy to do my spells and not calling on the divine. It has worked pretty d__n good too. But lately I've been exploring my spiritual side, I feel I've suppressed it a lot. So I just might start calling on divine beings, mending my relationship with god. But I will still be able to fall back on my other talents, energy magic and what not. This is just a new road for me, one I hope will lead me to a very spiritual life and a magical one at that too." GM

- "I am just learning how to do this stuff. I'm trying to contact my great-great-grandma Clara, so that I can learn of things she used. She used the power of the divine to heal and to accomplish many tasks. She would never take money. I recognize that other gods do exist, and they have their places in the universe. But there is one god at the top of the hierarchy for me." JJ

- "There was a time in my life when I referred to myself as a Christian witch. I no longer do so because I feel it is inaccurate in light of my beliefs, though they have changed very little. At the beginning of this year, I was baptized by water. It was necessary, as I did not feel I would be physically capable of leaving the sanctuary until I made that commitment to Christ, whose name I was using to describe my personal belief system. I am glad I did it. It was one of the most honest things I have ever done. I have accepted Jesus as my teacher and savior, for he has saved me from the mire of my own arrogance and ignorance. I follow his teachings to the best of my ability. I regard the rest of the Bible as a valuable reference on theological history, just as I regard all other religious texts. These days I make no claims to be anything other than an energy witch. I have had to admit to myself that I do not genuinely believe in any ALL-powerful being, and I am therefore certainly not a Christian in any sort of the accepted sense. Faith is a marvelous gift—one I hold in high regard. I do believe that a true faith in any thing lends validity to that thing's existence and empowers it." KA

- "Using aspects of Christianity is not in direct conflict with Witchcraft, unless you interpret that. They have miracles, we have outcomes. They have prayers, we have spells. It's all in the interpretation. I do not fear that I'm going to hell, because I am not Christian. But there are aspects of Christianity that can be incorporated into Witchcraft. I also don't believe that if you are a Christian that practices Witchcraft (which is not an oxymoron) that you will automatically go to hell." LD

- "I don't believe that god wants to crucify witches and he hates them, etc. He gave us free will to do what we want. He doesn't want to hurt you or damn you because you pursued another spiritual path. As long as you're not hurting anyone and you are being spiritual yourself, even though it might not be through him, I think he thinks it is all right." SX

It's all about building your own religion based on feelings, opinions, and experiences. In addition to having the choice to make up your own set of morals, Wicca also gives you the freedom to pick and choose what to believe and what to reject. Again, Wicca's high-profile flexibility regarding contrasting and even contradictory beliefs is highly appealing to those who prefer a self-styled belief system.

HAVE IT YOUR WAY

A popular fast-food restaurant chain tells its customers, "Have it your way." Wicca tells its followers the same thing. Maybe that's why it's so hard to define Wicca. There are some people who claim to be Wiccans who use the terms *Wicca* and *witchcraft* interchangeably. Then there are groups within witchcraft who follow the Wicca variety. Finally, there's the group that make a distinction between Wicca and witchcraft. Wiccans dislike any attempt to standardize their beliefs.

Wicca is a "buffet-style" religion and in a sense gives you the freedom to be your own god. It also appeals to our pride and natural rebellious spirit. According to mega-selling Wiccan author Scott Cunningham, there is not and can never be one "pure" or "true" or "genuine" form of Wicca. There are no central governing agencies, no physical leaders, no universally recognized prophets or messengers. Although specific, structured forms of Wicca certainly exist, they aren't in agreement regarding ritual, symbolism, and theology. Because of this healthy individualism, no one ritual or philosophical system has emerged to consume the others.[1]

Wicca, the religion of witches, is so self-styled that it's tough to get agreement on the exact and original meaning of the word *Wicca*. But this hasn't stopped teens from getting into the craft. It's a perfect fit for those who want a personally involving religion, celebrating both physical and spiritual realities, in which getting connected with deity is attached with the practice of magick. Most Wiccans or witches tend to worship nature, are experience oriented, do not believe in absolutes, and believe in many gods.

A big part of the attraction of the craft is their freedom to choose whom they worship. Naming a god is about what spiritually works for the individual. Some have compared the idea of Wiccan deities to a family tree (or pyramid), with the All, or universal energy. The All is basically a huge melting pot of all the gods everyone in the world has ever thought of or believed in.

The All is not male or female, has no body or real personality. It's more like a blender that you've dumped all the beliefs of the world into and crushed together. Travel down the pyramid, and the All divides

---

[1]Cunningham, *Wicca: A Guide for the Solitary Practitioner,* xi.

into two halves—female and male. The lord and the lady (god and goddess) symbolize the perfectly balanced male and female aspects of divinity that is vital to most Wiccans. Finally, closest to humans on earth, are the gods and goddesses. And just like you might choose a friend based on things that appeal to you instinctively or emotionally, so can Wiccans choose their favorite traits for a god and goddess.

There's no set of guidelines that dictates who or what the god and goddess must be; rather, there are ancient and symbolic descriptions of their essences and energies. The rest is left up to the individual Wiccans to design. The god can be tough or tender, fair-skinned or dark, long hair or short—whatever physicalities are desired.

But it doesn't stop here. There are also additional gods and goddesses that belong to a specific "pantheon" or group of deities that serve a particular people or culture, which a Wiccan can also add to their personal belief system. Some of the more common goddesses in Wicca are:

- Aphrodite: The Greek goddess of erotic love, beauty, and the feminine force. She symbolizes sensuality and feminine prowess.
- Aradia: This Italian goddess is also known as the Queen of Witches. She symbolizes the element of air and the moon.
- Bast: Also known as Baster, this is the Egyptian goddess of protection. She symbolizes cats, pleasure, childbirth, and the element of fire.
- Demeter: the Greek earth mother goddess. She symbolizes childbirth and protection.

Here are a few of the more common Wiccan male gods:

- Cernunnos: Also known as Herne the Hunter, this is the Celtic horned god. He symbolizes the hunt, male fertility, and animals. He is the most commonly worshiped god-form in Wicca. Wiccans claim that Cernunnos was part of the prototype for Christianity's Satan.
- Horus: The Egyptian god of the "all-seeing eye" who appears with the head of a falcon and the body of a man. He symbolizes light and healing.
- Mithra: The Persian sun god who is said to be the bringer of

light. He's a soldier's god who gives guidance and protection in battle. He symbolizes the element of air, fertility, and the mystery of magick.

- Taleisin: This Welsh god is a poet and harpist and is associated with wizards and sages.

There are so many deities in Wicca—and this is just the short list. It seems to me that it would be very confusing to know which god or goddess to turn to when you needed help. Amazingly, this aspect of Wicca seems to be appealing to teens in an attempt to get their "arms around spirituality" in a manageable way.

Psychic Michele Morgan, in her book *Simple Wicca*, says it's all about personal responsibility. "There's no confession or absolution of sins by an outside authority. Instead Wiccans are required to face up to their own actions, admit their mistakes and set things right whenever they can. Wiccans also believe in reincarnation, which deepens their commitment to personal and spiritual growth and to learning from all experiences."[2]

The craft encourages followers to develop a personal religious practice, gleaned from one's own experiences, wisdom, and instincts. Wiccans respect the idea that different spiritual beliefs work for different people. In fact, many witches add aspects of other religious systems, such as Native American Shamanism or Buddhism, to their rituals and practices. Others work closely with saints, angels, and even try to put Jesus into the mix. Religion is the language of spirituality, and Wiccans are definitely multilingual.[3]

One of the attractive things about Wicca is that there's no one right way to practice, worship, or believe. It's all about finding what fits for the individual—choosing what works for them spiritually—what they like, relate to, and identify with. Wicca is all about the individual being in control of one's own destiny. In an out-of-control world, do you think this appeals to your teen?

THE ONLY TRUE GOD

Surrender isn't a very popular word in our culture today—for teens or adults. Take, for example, all the hot spots globally where fighting is

---

[2]Morgan, 9.
[3]Ibid., 11–12.

taking place. Neither side wants to surrender, because that means they will lose. Or how about out on the highway—surrendering the right-of-way to another car? Are you kidding? Even if we're sitting in bumper-to-bumper traffic, something inside us says, "Don't give in to the car that's trying to merge in traffic from an on-ramp." But sometimes you don't have much choice when it comes to surrendering.

I travel a lot, which means I fly on quite a few airplanes. Every time I get on a plane I'm basically surrendering my life to the pilot. He or she is in charge of getting me where I need to go. There's no debating with him or her on which route I think they should take. When I step on that plane, I have decided to put my trust in that pilot to get me safely to my destination. And I have to admit there have been times that I've wondered if I made the right choice to trust a particular pilot—especially on some overseas flights. After one especially scary flight, as I was walking off the plane, the pilot smiled and said, "Cheated death once again!" That's not what you want to hear a pilot say!

Isn't it crazy how many times a week we put our trust in something or someone? When was the last time you tested your burger or burrito to see if it had been laced with poison? Or how about the chair you're sitting in—did you test it before you sat down to see if it would hold you? Unless you're really paranoid, you rarely stop to think about these kinds of things. So why is it so easy to surrender our will and put our trust in so many other people and things and not in God?

There are lots of reasons, but here are a few specific ones. First, you can't physically see God. But think about this: Have you ever seen the wind? Of course not, but you know it's there and you see the effects of it. Then there's the whole attitude of society that basically encourages us to be control freaks, especially when it comes to spirituality. But there is something else you may not have thought about—spiritual warfare and the devil. Wiccans say he doesn't exist, that he's a concept Christians have made up. But that isn't historically or biblically accurate. Think about it: If the devil is real, and he is our enemy, he definitely wouldn't want you to surrender your life to God and trust Him.

Wicca is leading a lot of teens—even those who attend church—down an empty and deceptive spiritual path. When you try to build your own religion and make your own gods, you put yourself in a dangerous position. What good is your religion or your god if they're no bigger than you? You're going to run out of energy, your wisdom is limited, as well as your personal resources. Whom do you turn to for help when your back is up against the wall? And how about love and forgiveness? How can you experience love from the moon, a rock, or some nebulous "universal energy" out in the cosmos somewhere? Or how about dealing with guilt? Wicca offers no real answers for any of these questions and more.

Habakkuk was a man who lived a long time ago in the Middle East. He had many of the same tough questions that we face today. And he wanted answers, just like you and I, so he boldly took his questions straight to God. And God answered him. Here's an answer Habakkuk received that speaks directly to Wicca and making up your own religion.

> What have you gained by worshiping all your man-made idols? How foolish to trust in something made by your own hands! What fools you are to believe such lies! How terrible it will be for you who beg lifeless wooden idols to save you. You ask speechless stone images to tell you what to do. Can an idol speak for God? They may be overlaid with gold and silver, but they are lifeless inside. (Habakkuk 2:18–19)

It doesn't get any clearer than that!

We don't really talk a lot about idolatry today, but it's more than just bowing down to some figurine or statue; it's trusting in what you've made, and therefore in your own power, as creator and sustainer. Do you trust in God or what your hands have made? Idols have no life, no personhood, no power. They're empty whether you're talking about something made of stone or a god or goddess you've created in your mind and on paper.

Let's think for a minute. Why would you want to worship a god that you created? That god would obviously be no greater or more powerful than you, so what help could it possibly be? The God of the Bible is sovereign—supreme, free from external control. He is all-powerful (see Psalm 139:13–16; Jeremiah 32:17; Psalm 115:3). Nothing is too hard for Him. God has the power and ability to see us through any situation in life. The opportunity to create your own deity may sound cool and fascinating, but in the end it's useless and dangerous to your soul.

When it comes to having the freedom to be yourself, the Bible contains a very interesting concept in John 8:32. It says that "you will know the truth, and the truth will set you free." Jesus himself is the source of truth. He does not give us the freedom to do what we want, but to do what God designed for us to do. The truth is that we all need a Savior because of our spiritual disease called sin. Jesus died on a cross to pay the penalty for our sin and set us free to be the people that we were created to be.

Christianity is not about a set of ideas that we buy into; it's about a relationship with a person—Jesus Christ. All other religions—including Wicca—tell us what we need to do. Christianity tells us what God has done for us. And remember, there's nothing you can do to earn this relationship—it's a free gift (Ephesians 2:8).

When we surrender our lives to Jesus, we become brand-new people. Check this out: "What this means is that those who become Christians become new persons. They are not the same anymore, for the old life is gone. A new life has begun!" (2 Corinthians 5:17). We're not rehabilitated or reeducated. We don't just change some stuff; we start a new life under a new Master.

But there's a catch—you have to surrender the old life for the new one. *Surrender* is a dirty word because the world says the way to freedom and becoming an individual is staying in charge.

When it comes to the kingdom of God, things are just the opposite. Jesus said, "If you try to keep your life for yourself, you will lose it. But if you give up your life for me, you will find true life" (Matthew 16:25). Surrendering isn't easy because you give up control. But because you're surrendering to the One who made you and knows what's best for you, you end up gaining a whole lot more than you give up.

WHAT'S IN IT FOR YOU?

So let's say you decide to surrender your life to Jesus; what's in it for you? Before we look at what you'll get, let's get a glimpse of what surrender will cost you.

To start with, basically everything. The Bible says, "God bought you with a high price" (1 Corinthians 6:20). The idea here is one of slaves being purchased at an auction. When Jesus died on the cross, He paid the penalty for our sins and set us free. What Jesus did was the ultimate demonstration of just how much God loves us (Romans 5:8). "This is real love. It is not that we loved God, but that he loved us and sent his Son as a sacrifice to take away our sins" (1 John 4:10). Because of what Jesus did, we are now obligated to serve Him. No place in Wicca will you find that a sacrifice of this significance was ever made by the All or the god and goddess.

Jesus explained the cost of following Him in this way: "If any of you wants to be my follower, you must put aside your selfish ambition, shoulder your cross, and follow me. If you try to keep your life for yourself, you will lose it. But if you give up your life for my sake and for the sake of the Good News, you will find true life" (Mark 8:34–35). The picture here is very vivid: If we want to follow Jesus, we must totally surrender to Him. God wants us to choose to follow Him and to stop trying to control our own destiny and let Him guide us. Once again, this makes good sense. Because God created us and absolutely loves us, He knows what real life is all about. Nothing will satisfy us like an intimate relationship with God.

Because of what God has done for us, He expects us to listen to Him, trust Him, and obey Him. And because of His great love for us, He has set up boundaries to help keep us on the right track and experience life the way He designed for us to. These boundaries, or commandments, are found throughout the Bible. For example, the Ten Commandments are found in Exodus 20. These commands, or guidelines, were meant to help us practically understand God's plan for us and how we should live. And because they come from God, we know they are good for us (Psalm 111:7).

I talk with a lot of teens who tell me they used to be Christians, but now they're into Wicca. I think what they're really saying is that they "used to go to church." I'm convinced that they never really had a relationship with God or understood what it's all about. If they really knew Jesus, and understood all that He has done for them, they never would have turned to Wicca. So what's it mean to be a follower of Jesus, and what are the benefits?

The first thing that most people think about when it comes to

Christianity is going to heaven when they die. Eternal life is definitely one of the benefits when you surrender your life to Jesus (John 6:40). Jesus gives us an incredible promise about heaven in John 14:2–3: "There are many rooms in my Father's home, and I am going to prepare a place for you. If this were not so, I would tell you plainly. When everything is ready, I will come and get you, so that you will always be with me where I am." Jesus is getting everything ready for us, and it's going to be greater than anything we can even imagine (1 Corinthians 2:7–9; Revelation 21:4). God's going to give us new bodies, and we will recognize and be able to spend time with friends and relatives who also trusted Christ (2 Corinthians 5:1; Matthew 17:3–4). What does Wicca offer that even comes close?

Wiccan philosophy embraces the concept of multiple reincarnations. Some Wiccans say that when we die, our soul journeys to a realm variously known as the Land of the Faerie, the Shining Land, and the Land of the Young. This realm is neither heaven nor the underworld. It simply is—a nonphysical reality much less dense than ours.[4] Others say our spirit is released back to the place they call Summerland.[5] Either way, they believe the soul needs some "continuing spiritual education," and when the time is right, another incarnation of the physical self takes place to go back to earth and continue to work out karma. Each body the soul inhabits on earth is different. No two bodies or lives are the same. This supposedly keeps the soul from getting stagnate. The sex, race, place of birth, economic class, and every other individuality of the soul is determined by its actions in past lives. Wiccan author Scott Cunningham writes, "There's no god or curse or mysterious force of fate upon which we thrust the responsibility for the trials in our lives. We decide what we need to learn in order to evolve, and then it is hoped, during incarnation, work toward this progress. If not, we regress into darkness."[6]

So what happens after the final incarnation? Wiccan teaching is pretty vague on this. But basically after rising up the spiral ladder of life and death and rebirth, Wiccans believe the souls who have attained perfection break away from the reincarnation/karma cycle and merge

---

[4]Cunningham, 71.
[5]Gary Cantrell, *Wiccan Beliefs and Practices* (St. Paul: Llewellyn Publications, 2003), 27.
[6]Cunningham, 70.

with the male and female balanced (god and goddess) creator entity.[7] *Stop and think. Reincarnation means that you keep paying for your sins over and over and over again.* After all this time, work, and energy, where is the hope of eternal life? And even more than that, the real you stopped existing somewhere in a past lifetime, so who is it that finally merges with a "force" out in the cosmos somewhere? Doesn't sound real appealing to me.

When you put the two side by side—Wicca and Christianity—there's no comparison. With Jesus there's no worrying about what happens when someone dies—God has guaranteed it! (John 10:28) But there's much more.

Skeptics usually say, "Big deal, you get a ticket to heaven—so what?" There's more to it, a lot more. There's eternal life with the Father. Remember Wiccans basically don't have a heaven, since most of them believe in reincarnation.

What are some other reasons you can give your teen that would make them want to surrender their life to Jesus—things that affect their life here on earth? Take a look at this list:

- All of your needs can be met (Psalm 34:10; Matthew 6:33)
- Wherever you go, whatever you do, you will be blessed (Deuteronomy 28:1–6)
- Forgiveness (Colossians 1:14)
- Help in times of trouble (Genesis 18:14; Psalm 118:5)
- Meaning in life (John 10:10)
- Adoption into God's family (John 1:12)
- Power to face challenges in life (Philippians 4:13)
- Peace (Philippians 4:7)
- Hope (Psalm 42:5; Hebrews 6:19)
- Direction for life (Psalm 25:8–11)
- Protection (Psalm 18:2–3)
- Purpose in life (Esther 4:13–14; Jeremiah 29:11)
- You are never alone (Hebrews 13:5)
- Joy to rise above your circumstances (John 15:11)
- Unconditional love (John 3:16; 13:27–28)

---

[7]Cantrell, 27.

Take a minute and let what you just read soak in—it's awesome! And it's not even close to all the benefits that are ours when we know God personally. What can Wicca offer that's even close? But your teen will never experience any of this by standing on the outside looking in. It's like standing outside a candy store and trying to imagine how sweet everything tastes.

Has your teen tasted Jesus, or are they still standing outside? They cannot know God until they enter into a personal relationship with Him through His Son, Jesus.

IT'S THEIR CHOICE

Neither you nor your teen will survive by trying to "have it your way." Eventually, you're going to get frustrated because things aren't working the way you want. Your teen can try to keep it together on his or her own, but they'll keep coming up empty-handed. But it's ultimately their decision, and they'll have no one to blame for the outcome except themselves. What they decide comes down to how they respond to these three questions:

- Do you trust the Bible?
- Does God exist?
- Who do you say Jesus is?

Their choice is to worship something they've created, or worship the Savior who created everything and understands us better than anyone ever could. He is intimately aware of how we're wired because He put us together. "You made all the delicate, inner parts of my body and knit me together in my mother's womb" (Psalm 139:13).

The God of the Bible is the only one who can satisfy your deepest needs and help you to become the person you were designed to be. But He expects total surrender. Help your teen choose wisely—the rest of his or her life on this planet and all of eternity is on the line.

CHAPTER 9:

WHY, GOD?

I HAD BEEN INVITED by the Billy Graham Evangelistic Association to speak at evangelistic meetings in New York for five days prior
to Mr. Graham's one-day event in Central Park. I assumed when I got
the call that I'd be speaking in auditoriums, gymnasiums, and small
arenas. But reality was quite different from my ideas—I was to speak at
street meetings in the Bronx! Up to this point in time I had done street
ministry overseas, but never in North America. What an experience!

I traveled with a small team of volunteers, and they gave me a
drum kit, sound system, and a banner to advertise the meeting in Central Park. We also brought a box full of literature with us. Early Monday
afternoon we set up across the street from the bus station. Our typical
approach to each meeting was to have me play a drum solo to draw a
crowd, then share a brief message, followed by an opportunity for
people to receive Christ. Then the volunteers and I would fan out
across the crowd and talk with people. After one particular meeting, I
had barely finished my brief message when an older African-American
woman—about half my size—came up to me. Before I could utter a
word, she started pounding on my chest, screaming, "If God is so good,
why did he let my five-year-old grandson get killed in a drive-by shooting?" What would you have said to her?

We live in a stressed-out, painful world that seems to move from one tragedy to another. There are natural disasters like earthquakes, hurricanes, fires, and floods.

After the deadly tsunami hit Southeast Asia in December 2004, people of all faiths were asking, "Why us? Why here? Why now?" You could say this cataclysm was of biblical proportions, but most of the Hindus, Muslims, and Buddhists who were caught up in the disaster and survived had never heard the story of Noah and the God of wrath.[1] Christians familiar with the Bible were reminded of the story of Job in the Old Testament. He lost everything and was tested to the extreme. But even the account of Job doesn't seem to answer the timeless questions about why bad things happen or why a loving God can or would allow such suffering.

To followers of Wicca, earthquakes and tidal waves are simply a case of mother nature stretching. "She had a kink in her back and stretched," states Ruth Barrett, a Wiccan high priestess who formerly led a group in Los Angeles and now heads a Wisconsin temple dedicated to the Roman goddess Diana. Though the resulting casualties were horrendous, she said that dwelling on why people suffered was narcissistic when nature constantly reshapes itself. "We're so self-centered and think we are the be-all and end-all of the universe," she said.[2] Priestess Barrett doesn't seem to have many answers from her Wiccan beliefs for this tragedy.

What do you think about disasters like the tsunami? How do you explain what happened? What about suffering in your own life or that of a friend or co-worker—do you ever feel like shaking your fist at the sky and saying, "God, where are you?"

One in ten American women takes an antidepressant drug, and the use of such drugs by all adults has nearly tripled in the last decade, according to the federal government's latest figures on American health.[3] Clearly we're struggling to handle the pain.

If we as adults are undergoing such pain and stress, we can be sure the difficulty is even greater for teenagers what with so many questions and pressures facing them today. The number of children getting

---

[1]Kenneth L. Woodward, "Countless Souls Cry Out to God," *Newsweek*, January 10, 2005, 37.
[2]Teresa Watanabe and Larry B. Stammer, "Deadly Tsunami Resurrects the Old Question of Why," *Los Angeles Times*, Saturday, January 8, 2005, B2.
[3]Shankar Vedantam, "Antidepressant Use by U.S. Adults Soars," *Washington Post*, Friday, December 3, 2004, A15.

psychiatric drugs has also soared. In 2002, about 6 percent of all boys and girls were taking antidepressants; triple the rate in the period between 1994 and 1996.[4]

There are an awful lot of people inside and outside of the church that are angry with God because of situations in their lives.

Wicca embraces those who have turned bitter toward God and those who are disillusioned over not obtaining answers to their prayers or seeing friends and family members suffer.

Josh is fifteen years old and says he's a Wiccan. He used to believe in God, but doesn't anymore. Wicca suits him much better. He likes being earth-friendly and being able to have a religion that's more comfortable. Besides, if God really cared about him, his mother would still be alive today. But ever since Josh turned his back on God and started practicing Wicca, he still doesn't seem to have a lot of answers about his mom's death and other difficult stuff in his life.

Everyone wonders why a loving God would allow evil to flourish in our world. Wicca answers that question by promising its believers the power to set things right. But in some cases the cost may be higher than what you expect. And where does the power come from?

Two good friends got involved in the craft and decided to pursue another path to find answers about the tough stuff in life. Investigators in Knox, Kentucky, say they may never know what sparked the suicides of Sarah Casey and Debra Kawaguchi. Investigators maintain that the teenage girls deliberately walked together onto railroad tracks and into the path of an oncoming train on Saturday morning, August 28. But the "why" remains unknown.

In an effort to make sense of it all, investigators have been looking into all of the girls' interests. Officials found that they were both interested in Wicca. Detective Oscar Cowen of the Starke County Sheriff's Department said, "The girls may have latched on to some notion of reincarnation and, not understanding what death means, made an ill-informed decision to end their own lives in hopes of returning as better people."[5]

It appears as if no one told Sarah and Debra that suicide is a per-

---

[4]Ibid.

[5]Joshua Stowe, "Officials Seek Answers in Teens' Deaths," (Indiana: *South Bend Tribune* newspaper—online edition—*www.southbendtribune.com*, September 1, 2004).

manent solution to temporary problems.

How do you handle the pain and suffering of life? There are so many kinds of suffering—abuse, rejection, loneliness, diseases like cancer, physical disabilities, emotional struggles, or the death of a friend or family member. Where do you turn for help?

There are answers that I've personally found and experienced. They didn't come easy, but it was worth it.

TOUGH LESSONS

It was a little after 7:00 A.M. when my friends Chuck and Jamie headed west on Highway 58 after traveling up Highway 395. They were part of our ministry team and on their way to central California for some final meetings in preparation for a citywide evangelistic event we were having the following week in Madera. A few minutes later, at approximately seven-thirty that morning, Chuck and Jamie were hit head on by another vehicle speeding at one hundred miles per hour on the wrong side of the road.

Chuck was killed instantly—the steering wheel of the small truck crushed his chest. The paramedics were able to get Jamie into an ambulance, but he died on the way to the hospital. The four guys in the other car walked away from the accident—they were stone drunk and not injured. I didn't hear about the accident until Chuck's pastor called our office at three o'clock that afternoon. In disbelief I kept telling some of our staff members that the pastor was wrong because Chuck and Jamie were supposed to call me around three-thirty. I was numb and couldn't believe that something this awful could happen.

Over the course of the weeks following the accident I found myself feeling hurt, confused, and angry with God. I'd be crying—which is very unusual for me—then looking up to the sky and yelling, "God— why? Why did Chuck and Jamie have to die?" I reminded God that they were good guys—husbands, fathers—and faithfully serving Him. "What gives, God? How could you let something like this happen?" I wasn't getting anywhere except feeling more and more frustrated. It came down to a choice: I was either going to turn to God to see if He had any answers, or walk away. I decided to dig into the Bible to see if I had missed something. Here are a few of the lessons I learned about pain and suffering after the death of my good friends.

First, God is in control. He is sovereign (Jeremiah 1:6), which means He's free from any external control; He is supreme, excellent, and powerful. We've got to realize that we will never be able to find an explanation for all the things that happen in life. "God has made everything beautiful for its own time. He has planted eternity in the human heart, but even so, people cannot see the whole scope of God's work from beginning to end" (Ecclesiastes 3:11). And we have to learn that God's thoughts are nothing like ours and His ways are beyond what we could even imagine (Isaiah 55:8). We may never know why something has happened; instead, ask God, "What next?" and "How can I best navigate through the troubled waters of my life?"

When you're going through a tough time, do you focus on the circumstances or on God? Our natural tendency is to look for a quick fix, but sometimes God doesn't work as fast as we would like Him to. Don't bail on Him; instead, try to focus on how awesome and powerful He is. The same power that God used to create the heavens and the earth (Genesis 1–2) and to raise Jesus from the dead (Acts 2:32) is available to help you with even the most difficult circumstances in your life.

The next lesson I learned is that pain and suffering are a natural part of life. Living in the United States we can have a distorted picture about the goodness of God. We tend to think that it means possessing a lot of material stuff and experiencing no problems. And up until 9/11, most Americans felt sheltered and protected. It's kind of like, "If we don't do anything real bad, then everything will be fine." But that's not what God says in the Bible. Suffering is an intrusion in God's original design of creation (Genesis 1:31). It's not what He desired. Suffering is a result of sin—trying to live our lives without God. And it all started way back with the first man and woman in the Garden of Eden (Genesis 3:16–19).

Adam and Eve chose to disobey God (sin). They bought the lie from Satan—who was disguised as a serpent. The lie: "You can be god of your own life." People are still being deceived like this today through Wicca. Because God is holy, He had to respond in a way consistent with His perfect moral nature. He had to punish their sin. The consequences of Adam and Eve's sin may seem extreme, but remember their sin set in motion humanity's tendency toward disobeying God. Every person who was ever born—except Jesus—has been born with a sinful nature (Romans 5:12–21), and as a result pain and suffering became a natural part of life.

God views sin of any kind very seriously. Even in small amounts, sin can prove to be toxic and deadly to our lives. But amazingly, even when we do disobey Him, God is still willing to forgive us. That's something that Wicca doesn't offer.

Jesus promised us that if we followed Him, we would experience pain and suffering. "I have told you all this so that you may have peace in me. Here on earth you will have many trials and sorrows. But take heart, because I have overcome the world" (John 16:33). Jesus wants us to be confident and brave. In spite of the inevitable struggles we will face, He wants us to know that we will never be alone. Jesus does not abandon us in our pain and struggles. He has already won the ultimate victory—over death—when He died on the cross. So we can have His peace even in the toughest times.

And as hard as it may be to understand, God has a purpose in our pain and suffering. Check this out: "Dear brothers and sisters, whenever trouble comes your way, let it be an opportunity for joy. For when your faith is tested, your endurance has a chance to grow" (James 1:2–3). Notice this verse doesn't say *if* trouble comes, but *when* it does. We're going to have troubles, and it's possible to benefit from them. We're not supposed to pretend that we are happy when we are in pain; instead, God wants us to have a positive attitude because of what struggles can produce in our life. We need to turn our times of pain into times of learning. These tough times can teach us perseverance. Once you can get the picture that suffering is part of life, then you can realize the importance of perseverance.

You may not be experiencing pain in your life right now, but eventually you will. Then what? How will you cope?

Finally, when we're facing difficult times, we need to trust in God and His character. In what I've experienced, I've realized that it's one thing to stand in front of an audience or talk about this subject on the radio, but it's much different when you are clinging to God's promises yourself because of the pain you're going through. I can tell you from personal experience that God is faithful, even in the darkest times. God is powerful and completely loving, not a cowering genie in a bottle—a mystical, impersonal force out in the cosmos somewhere.

From generation to generation God has revealed himself as a personal God who wants an intimate relationship with His people. He wants us to see Him, know Him, and speak with Him, and as a result ultimately to trust Him. And when we do trust Him, God promises to help us. "Do not be afraid or discouraged, for the Lord is the one who will go before you. He will be with you; he will neither fail you nor forsake you" (Deuteronomy 31:8). Check out this promise in Job. "But by means of their suffering, he rescues those who suffer. For he gets their attention through adversity" (36:15).

Sometimes God uses pain and suffering as a form of discipline we need to get back on the right track (Psalm 119:67, 71, 75; Hebrews 12:6–10; 1 Corinthians 11:31–32). Most of the time He uses it to help us grow stronger and build character in our lives (Proverbs 25:4). God wants us to become better, not bitter about the circumstances in our lives. And don't forget, He always does what is best for us. "And we know that God causes everything to work together for the good of those who love God and are called according to his purpose" (Romans 8:28). This verse doesn't mean that everything that happens to us is good, because there *is* evil in the world. But God does work for our good in everything—every situation—not just in isolated situations. And remember, because He is God, He sees the big picture of our lives—beginning to end.

The best way to practically apply these lessons is through prayer. Wiccans would call it using the cone of power. Take Wayne, a high school student who sent me the following e-mail:

> "The 'cone' of power is no different than Christian prayer. You ask God for help to cure your cancer-stricken mother; you focus your mind to attain this end. You want it with your whole body and soul because you love her and want her to be well. What is so wrong with that? Because people do not pray to your specific God they are wrong and are going to an eternal damnation? If that is what your 'loving God' is like, I want nothing to do with Him."

In actuality, the cone of power is *very* different from prayer. The cone of power is a method of directing the energy of an individual or group for a singular purpose or to provide a connection to spirit. This energy is a combination of love, creativity, and spirit, and forms the basis for a witch's power, which he or she raises to accomplish a desire. A witch builds up energy by chanting and swaying. Once the heat from the energy has reached a certain level, it must be directed into a magickal tool or objective, where it can be held. At the desired time the energy can be sent out to achieve the desired result.

When Christians pray, we are asking God for help because we recognize that we have no power or ability in ourselves to affect a change in a situation or help someone. It is not a matter of focusing our mind on a particular end, but rather demonstrating our total dependence upon God to act, according to His will. The God of the Bible is a God of love and wants the best for each one of us, and that includes securing our eternal destiny in heaven. He made this possible through Jesus' death on the cross.

Prayer in its simplest form is having a conversation with God—talking to Him, then quietly listening and waiting for His answer. In all the years that I've been following Jesus, I've never heard an audible voice from the sky. But my prayers have been answered in a variety of ways—including "No." That's the hard part—trusting that God loves me so much that He will always do what is best for me in every situation—if I depend on Him. That's where faith comes in. "Faith . . . is the confident assurance that what we hope for is going to happen. It is the evidence of things we cannot yet see" (Hebrews 11:1). The beginning point of faith is believing in God's character: that He is who He says.

But the Bible teaches that God has only committed himself to answer the prayers of His children. "The eyes of the Lord watch over those who do right, and his ears are open to their prayers. But the Lord turns his face against those who do evil" (1 Peter 3:12). That could be one reason why you have not experienced answers to your prayers—you have not put your faith and trust in Jesus. God has chosen to do nothing for us until we let Him do something in us.

If you have not accepted Christ, then the next chapter, "Fact, Fiction, or Feeling," is for you. Pay careful attention to what you read.

A PARTNER FOR LIFE

There is help and hope in the midst of pain and suffering—it's found in the person of Jesus. "Come to me, all of you who are weary and carry heavy burdens, and I will give you rest. Take my yoke upon you. Let me teach you, because I am humble and gentle, and you will find rest for your souls. For my yoke is easy to bear, and the burden I give you is light" (Matthew 11:28–30).

A yoke is a heavy wooden harness that fits over the shoulders of an ox or oxen, and it's attached to a piece of equipment that the ox or oxen pull. Are you pulling a heavy load around? It could be any number of things—bad health, being a victim of downsizing at work, a broken marriage, rejection, unconfessed sin, or even weariness in your search for God. Jesus can free you from these burdens. The rest He promises is love, healing, and peace with God. But it doesn't mean the end of problems or hard work. The difference is that with Jesus we don't face the difficulties alone, because now the weight of our pain falls on His shoulders, which are much bigger than ours.

Whatever pain and suffering you are facing, don't go through it alone. Put aside your misconceptions about God and let Him take over. Make Jesus your first resource rather than your last resort. It won't be easy, but it will be worth it. When pain and suffering hit your life, and doubts begin to flood your mind and heart, put your confidence in God and don't give up!

CHAPTER 10:

FACT, FICTION, OR FEELING: WHOSE WORD ARE YOU GOING TO TRUST?

THE DAVINCI CODE by Dan Brown is a fast-paced, fascinating suspense novel that debuted as number one on the *New York Times* bestseller list. It sold an amazing six million copies within one year after it was published. It was subsequently translated into forty languages.

Despite the fact that it's a fiction book, many people who are reading it have started to question all they have ever believed about Jesus Christ, the Bible, and the early Christian church. In what many have referred to as a "harmless novel," it describes alleged historical facts that call into question many things that are foundational to Christianity. For example: Did early church leaders really believe that Jesus was divine? Is it possible that Jesus and Mary Magdalene were not only married but also had a daughter? According to Brown's book, these and other secrets have been carefully kept hidden through the centuries of conspiracy by the Christian church so it could keep control of its huge power base.

On one hand Brown claims his book is pure fiction, but he also claims it's based on real historical facts about art, architecture, secret rituals, and underground societies. Yet in the book Brown also contradicts the biblical view of sexuality, the esteem of women, and the divinity of Christ. He actually calls Jesus a "mortal prophet." Brown believes the Bible is a product of man and therefore flawed. He is a proponent of Gnosticsm (a group of ancient heresies stressing escape from this world through the attainment of mysterious knowledge). Gnostics would say that Jesus came not to set us free from our sin but to free us from our ignorance. He brings us knowledge (gnosis) that we are divine.

The DaVinci Code is really much more than a neutral novel with a few facts thrown in—it's propaganda for a religious world view based on the worship of nature and the goddess. If it comes down to one against the other, whose word are you going to trust—God's or Dan's?

Wiccan psychic Michele Morgan wants to help her readers understand simply what she calls a complex religion, science, art, and way of life. "It is my desire to simplify what can seem positively overwhelming by taking you out of the 'head' and into the 'heart' of the Wiccan way. If you experience something first, it can be far easier to assimilate the myriad details that go into creating it."[1]

While these people may mean well and want to help others find a way to make sense out of life, where are the facts? Everything they believe and write is based on feelings and experiences. Obviously, these are both elements of spirituality, but there's more to it. Do you really want to base the rest of your life and your eternal destiny on someone's feelings and experiences? Whose word are you going to trust? There's too much at stake to be that careless and haphazard.

In this chapter I will challenge you to set aside your prejudices— things you've heard from friends, co-workers, relatives, and even some things you may have read about God, Jesus, and the Bible from authors like those mentioned above. I want you to think. See if you can connect the "dots" of information.

The truths found on the next few pages are among the most important you'll ever encounter. These are the answers God has given us in response to our deepest questions.

---

[1] Morgan, xi.

THE BIBLE

The Bible is not a collection of stories, myths, fables, or simple human ideas about God. It's not a human book. In 2 Timothy 3:16 we read, "All Scripture is inspired by God and is useful to teach us what is true and to make us realize what is wrong in our lives. It straightens us out and teaches us to do what is right." In other words, the Bible is literally God-breathed. Inspiration can be defined as the mysterious process by which God worked through human writers. They wrote from their own personal, historical, and cultural context. And even though the writers used their own minds, talents, and language, they wrote what God wanted them to write. The Bible is free from any errors in its original writings.

But be careful how you use and understand the term *inspiration*. Usually we think of a singer, author, or artist being "inspired" in their work, which means we think it's really good. But when this same word is applied to the Bible, it has a different meaning. The Bible has been "breathed" by God. The Bible claims to be His very Word: it has come from His very mouth.[2] No other religious book has ever made this claim, nor is it as historically reliable as the Bible. The authors of the Bible—most of them prophets—spoke God's words. A prophet was someone who was supposed to say exactly what God told him to say (Jeremiah 26:2; Exodus 4:30). God didn't verbally dictate the Bible to each author; yet the end result is just as precise as if He had. God supernaturally supervised what they wrote, and because God was in control of its writing, the Bible is completely trustworthy.

The Bible is the most unique book ever written. It's the written Word of God. The Bible was written over a fifteen-hundred-year span of time, by forty-four different authors—all living in different places— in three different languages (Hebrew, Aramaic, and Greek), on three different continents (Asia, Africa, and Europe). It's an amazing book in its unity in the midst of its vast diversity. The Bible has one continuous drama from Genesis to Revelation—the rescue of humanity. It has a central theme—the person of Jesus Christ. And from the beginning to the end, the Bible has one unified message: Humanity's problem is sin

---

[2]Josh McDowell, *The New Evidence That Demands a Verdict* (Nashville: Thomas Nelson, 1999), 334.

and the remedy is found in Jesus. All this evidence points to the idea that there was one mind behind the writing of the Bible—God's.

The uniqueness of the Bible's message can be summed up in Romans 6:23: "For the wages is sin is death, but the free gift of God is eternal life through Christ Jesus our Lord." Christianity teaches that all people enter this world spiritually dead and choose sin by default (Romans 3:23); we are separated from God because of sin, and there is no possibility that we can fix ourselves (Ephesians 2:8–9). Other religions may agree there is something spiritually wrong with us, but they hold out hope that somehow, through some kind of human effort, we can make it right.

But even though the Bible rejects this and says we have a humanly irreparable spiritual condition, there is truly good news—God has a remedy. We can have eternal life—not just some continued existence on another spiritual plane after death; we can actually have fellowship with God himself (John 17:3). No other religion in the world promises us eternal life and closeness with the living God (Hebrews 4:16). And it starts in this life—the moment we place our faith and trust in Jesus Christ. Finally, this message is unique because eternal life is a free gift. It's not something that can be earned; it can only be received. We can have this gift by admitting our need for life because of our spiritual death—and then relying on the work that Jesus did for us by paying the penalty for our sin.

But these are not the only reasons why the Bible is so unique. For example, no other book ever written has had the kind of circulation the Bible has had. Billions of copies have been sold and distributed around the world. The Bible was also one of the first important books ever translated. According to the United Bible Societies, the Bible (and portions of it) has been translated into more than twenty-two hundred languages.

The Bible is also unique in its ability to have survived over the course of time, through countless attempts at destruction and persecution. It actually has more ancient manuscript evidence to support it than any ten pieces of classical literature combined.[3] Throughout history people have tried to burn and outlaw the Bible. Others have spent

---

[3]Ibid., 9.

their lives trying to refute it—even so-called scholars. Yet the Bible has endured all its enemies and has been able to stand up to even the most persistent critics.

When tested by the same criteria by which other historical manuscripts are tested, the Bible demonstrates incredible accuracy for the historical events it reports. For example, did you know that there are 5,656 partial and complete manuscript portions (in Greek) of just the New Testament alone? In comparison, the next closest historical manuscript is Homer's *Iliad*, with only 643 copies. Then we need to consider supporting evidence that comes from sources like early Christian writers outside the Bible like Clement of Rome, Ignatius, or Polycarp. Or consider support from non-Christian historical writers like Tacitus and Josephus.

Think about the Bible's prescient statements about the earth, the heavens, and humanity that predate their discoveries by anywhere from two to three millennia. For example, look at what God said in Leviticus 3:17. "You must never eat any fat or blood. This is a permanent law for you and all your descendents, wherever they may live." Think about it. It took us thirty-five hundred years and lots of doctor bills to find out that animal fats are the heaviest in cholesterol.

Or what about the concept of allowing the ground to remain unplowed and unused during every seventh year (Exodus 23:10–11)? Scientists have now discovered that this concept, which allow enzymes to renew themselves so they can carry on for another six years, was accurate and way ahead of its time.

In the 1840s pregnant women had a one-in-six rate of dying from "childbirth fever" if they went to a particular hospital in Vienna, Austria. Dr. Ignaz Semmelweis noticed something in common about their deaths. Doctors who had just completed an autopsy on victims of "childbirth fever" had examined all the women who died. So Dr. Semmelweis implemented a new policy that all doctors must wash their hands after performing an autopsy. As a result, the death rate among pregnant women dropped radically to one in eighty-four. What's significant about this story is that God set down cleanliness laws through Moses thirty-five hundred years before Dr. Semmelweis's policy on doctors' washing their hands (Numbers 19:17, 19).

We also need to examine archaeological evidence that supports the

Bible. Well-known archaeologist Nelson Glueck said, "It may be stated categorically that no archaeological discovery has ever controverted a biblical reference. Scores of archaeological findings have been made which conform in clear outline or exact detail historical statements in the Bible."[4] There can be no question as to the historical reliability of the Bible.

The Bible is unique because it is the only book in the world ever written to offer specific predictions about the future, hundreds of years in advance, that were literally fulfilled. A lot of these predictions focus on the first and second coming of Christ. There are several unique things about prophecies in the Bible in contrast to other attempts made to predict the future events:

- The prophecies were very specific.
- None of these predictions ever failed.
- Since the prophecies about Christ were written hundreds of years before His birth, no one could have even been making intelligent guesses.
- Many of these predictions were beyond human ability to somehow force fulfillment.

The best way to explain how all this was possible is the existence of a living God who knows all things—the beginning from the end (Isaiah 46:10).

When you hear some psychic on TV or read your so-called prophecy on a magazine cover at the market, remember a very important test for false prophets—whether all of their predictions come to pass (Deuteronomy 18:22). In biblical times, those whose predictions failed were stoned to death (Deuteronomy 18:20). If that happened today, it would cause some serious hesitation on the part of some people—maybe even cause them to find another line of work! No true biblical prophet made even a single prophetic error.

Another sure way of distinguishing true prophets from false ones is by miracles (Acts 2:22; Hebrews 2:3–4). Miracles are confirmation that a prophet is actually speaking for God, because they are supernatural acts of God. And if you examine all the other religious leaders in the

---

[4]Dean C. Halverson, *The Compact Guide to World Religions* (Minneapolis: Bethany House Publishers, 1996), 256.

world, you will find that only the Judeo-Christian leaders were super-naturally confirmed by genuine miracles that couldn't possibly be some form of mental or emotional experience or some kind of trickery. Moses, Elijah, Paul, and Peter performed miraculous signs among the people (Exodus 4:1; 1 Kings 18; Acts 2:4; 3:1–10; 20:10). But more importantly, the ministry of Jesus was marked and accredited by God through miracles, signs, and wonders (Acts 2:22).

We could talk about the Bible's unique impact on civilization, as well as on literature. But we must also recognize its unique teachings on character, history, and prophecy. It's amazing when you consider all the future events throughout history that have occurred, which were predicted in the Bible hundreds, sometimes even thousands, of years in advance. No unconditional prophecy of the Bible about events to the present day has gone unfulfilled. Other books claim divine inspiration, such as the Koran, the Book of Mormon, and parts of the (Hindu) Veda. But none of those books contains predictive prophecy that is completely accurate.[5] Hundreds of predictions—at times given hundreds of years in advance—have been literally fulfilled. Fulfilled prophecy is another glaring sign of the unique divine authority of the Bible.

The Bible is our ultimate source of truth. It doesn't make any sense why anyone would want to base his or her eternal destiny—and life on the planet—purely on someone's opinions, feelings, or experiences when we have God's Word—the Bible—available to help us and guide us. The core message of the Bible, which sets it apart from any other book in all of history, is the offer of the free gift of eternal life through Jesus Christ.

Use the Bible as God intended—as an immovable anchor for your life.

GOD

Bruce Almighty, a movie starring Jim Carrey, is a story about a local TV news reporter who is discontented with nearly everything in his life, and he rarely misses an opportunity to complain about it. After being fired from his job and having the worst day of his life, Bruce rages and rails against the Lord for his rotten luck. He then experiences

[5]Ibid., 12.

a series of curious signs, which eventually lead him to an old building where he meets a nondescript janitor (Morgan Freeman) who ultimately reveals that he is God. He's heard Bruce's complaints and now has an offer for the choleric newscaster—His job!

God gives Bruce all His powers and challenges him to take on the big job to see if he can do any better. Bruce proceeds to utilize these infinite powers for his own amusement, advancement, and advantage until he finally stands at a crossroads. He must decide whether or not he will become the biggest jerk in the universe or find a little bit of humanity in "Bruce Almighty."

Once again Hollywood has given us an interesting look at God and what He might be like. Curious as it may be to think about God giving away His power, it's far from the truth and nowhere close to reality. So what about God—does He really exist? And if He does, what's He like?

There are those in Wicca who teach that it's ultimately up to each person to decide whether the Divine is one great power or many. They also say that it's a personal thing as to what characteristics of the god, goddess, or other deities, witches look to for guidance and support in their daily spiritual journey. We talked a lot about this earlier in chapter 8, "Religion Any Way You Want It."

So how do we know that God exists? Are there valid reasons for believing, or are we supposed to accept Him by blind faith?

Your entire life on earth and after death is affected by whether you see yourself as god of your life or if you acknowledge and submit to the living God—one who is to be respected and loved.

What evidence is there for God? To begin with, you can't examine Him in a test tube or prove Him with usual scientific methodology. However, we can say with equal emphasis that it's not possible, by scientific method, to prove that the French general Napoleon ever lived. The reason lies in the nature of history itself and in the limitations of the scientific method.[6] In order for something to be proved scientifically, it must be repeatable. History is not repeatable. That something or someone cannot be repeated does not disprove their reality, so it's irrational to suggest that somehow the reality of God can or should be proved scientifically.

---

[6]Paul E. Little, *Know Why You Believe* (Downers Grove, IL: InterVarsity Press, 2000), 23.

Those who work in the field of anthropology have indicated that there is a universal belief in God among the most remote peoples of the globe today. In the earliest histories and legends of peoples all around the world, the original concept was that of one God, who is Creator. An original high God appears to have been in their conscious-ness even in those societies that are today polytheistic.[7] It is increasingly clear that the oldest traditions everywhere were of one supreme God.[8]

Brilliant men throughout history have concluded this very thing. Augustine said, "Our hearts are restless until they can rest in thee." The great seventeenth-century mathematician, Blaise Pascal, talked about the "God-shaped vacuum" in the heart of each person. Centuries ago Solomon, thought to be the wisest man to ever live, wrote these words: "God has made everything beautiful for its own time. He has planted eternity in the human heart, but even so, people cannot see the whole scope of God's work from beginning to end" (Ecclesiastes 3:11).

It's the law of cause and effect. There's graffiti on the walls at school; someone painted it—the stuff didn't just appear. There's a tree in your front yard—it must have been planted there. Nothing comes from nothing. From the beginning of human existence, we as people— our beings—had to have a cause. So do this planet and the rest of the universe. *The cause is God.* Where, then, did God originate? He didn't. God is eternal . . . self-existent . . . uncreated. Everything else that lives has life because God *is*.

Look at it another way. The computer that I used to write this book could not have been made without an intelligent designer; it was never going to combine and appear by random chance. Or how about some-thing else even more complex—our bodies. Stop reading right now and go look in a mirror. Think logically: We couldn't possibly have evolved from a single cell in the bottom of a streambed somewhere to eventu-ally become this incredibly fine-tuned, intricate organism that we are, without an intelligent designer or creator.

Or what about the design and order of the universe? Think about the planets and the stars—about their placement in the heavens, their function, and the position of the earth. If the earth were any closer to the sun, we'd all be crispy critters. If we were any farther away, we'd

[7]Ibid.

[8]Samuel Zwemer, *The Origin of Religion* (Neptune, NJ: Loizeaux Bros., 1945), n.p.

all be blocks of ice. Or how about gravity? Everything in life screams out that someone must have put everything together and is maintaining it.

Consider another piece of evidence for God's existence. C. S. Lewis talks about "right and wrong being a clue to the meaning of the universe." Inside of each one of us is a command or influence trying to get us to behave in a certain way.[9] People basically appeal to some sense of right and wrong. For example, I have received a lot of e-mails from Wiccans wanting to know why Christians just can't accept the Wiccan religion. Something inside of them is triggering this desire to be accepted and do what's right. You can see this in a variety of ways in even the smallest activities of life. It comes down to a sense of what ought to take place. It's more than just cultural norms; it's morals. So if there is a moral law inside of each of us, there must be a moral lawgiver. The Bible says that we are made in God's image, setting us apart from all other creation. No other part of creation will ever discuss what is right or wrong. Ever hear this coming from a tree, a rock, or how about a dog or cat? There is somebody behind the universe. He is God—who has a mind, emotions, conscience, and will—a complete personality.[10] "They demonstrate that God's law is written within them, for their own consciences either accuse them or tell them they are doing what is right" (Romans 2:15).

One final piece of evidence to consider is God's presence in the changed lives of people. When someone puts his or her faith and trust in Jesus Christ, there is an incredible change that takes place in an individual's life. Think about stories you have heard about people going through unbelievable tragedy or trials in life and God has given them strength, peace, and hope. Why are people all over the globe today giving up everything to follow Jesus?

Each one of us must decide: Do we believe that the human race and the universe just happened, or is it the result of divine design by an all-knowing and all-powerful God?

The Bible never makes an effort to prove that God exists; it assumes that He always has. The terms used to describe what God is like are called attributes. When you begin to grasp these descriptive character-

---

[9]Little, 32.
[10]Ibid., 33.

istics of God, you will see another reason why Christianity is so unique compared to other religions in the world. So what is God really like?

- God is all-powerful (omnipotent). It is His power that created the earth and everything in it (Job 42:2; Psalm 115:3; Jeremiah 32:17; Mathew 19:26).
- God is all-knowing (omniscient). He is familiar with all our thoughts and actions and has the answers to the issues of life (Psalm 139:1–6; Isaiah 46:9–10; John 2:25).
- God is changeless (immutable). God is not subject to changes in society or culture; He always remains the same (Psalm 102:27; Hebrews 13:8; James 1:17).
- God is perfection (holiness). God has no equal in holiness; He alone is the standard of ethical purity (Exodus 15:11; Psalm 24:3; Isaiah 40:25; Habakkuk 1:13).
- God is timeless (eternal). He has no beginning and no end. There's never been a time when He has not existed (Deuteronomy 33:27; Isaiah 44:6, 57:15; John 5:26).
- God is unlimited (infinite). He is not confined by the universe or time-space boundaries (1 Kings 8:27; 2 Chronicles 2:6; Psalm 147:5; Jeremiah 23:24; Acts 17:24–28).
- God is separate from His creation (transcendent—above and beyond). He is the source of all life and is self-existing (Isaiah 57:15).
- God is also present in His creation (immanent—near to) (Isaiah 57:15).
- God is in all places at all times (omnipresent). He is completely present everywhere. God is with you no matter where you go. There is no place where God cannot be found (Psalm 139:7–12; Jeremiah 23:23–24).
- God is spirit. He is not composed of matter and does not possess a physical nature. Even though He is a spirit—without a physical body—God is still very real (Psalm 145:13; John 1:18, 4:24; 1 Timothy 1:17, 6:15–16).
- God is personal. He is an individual being, with self-consciousness and will, capable of feeling, choosing, and having a reciprocal relationship with other personal and social beings.[11]

[11]Erickson, 295.

We can learn more about God's personality in the Bible. Begin with the fact that God has a name. In Exodus 3:14, He identifies himself as "I AM." This shows us that He is not just some nameless force floating around in the universe. Another sign of God's personal nature is His activity, especially knowing and interacting with people—humans. This developed early in His relationship with humankind—regular talks with Adam and Eve in Genesis 3. He has all the capabilities associated with personality: knowing, feeling, willing, and acting. God sees, hears, speaks, and remembers (Numbers 11:1; 2 Timothy 2:19).

- God is love (all-loving). His love is perfect because it is divine. God's love can be seen throughout the Bible, beginning to end. This is the very nature of God. God's love is a rational and voluntary affection, not just some emotional impulse. Ultimately, "God is love" was expressed through Jesus in His three years of ministry, peaking with His death on the cross. "For God so loved the world that he gave his only Son, so that everyone who believes in him will not perish but have eternal life" (John 3:16). (See also Hosea 11:4; Jeremiah 31:3; Mark 1:41, 10:16; Luke 15:1; 1 John 4:8, 10.)

- God is truth. By definition truth means that the facts conform to reality; truth identifies things as they are.[12] He is the one true God distinct from all others; there is no other like Him. His Word—the Bible—is reliable and therefore He can be trusted. God is the source of all truth, the beginning of all knowledge, and He makes it available to us so we can have a relationship with Him. (See Isaiah 44:8–10, 45:5; Numbers 23:19; Romans 3:3–4; John 14:1, 2, 6; Hebrews 6:18; Titus 1:2.)

You've just read a lot of biblical support for belief in God. And based on what you read earlier in this chapter, you know that the Bible is more reliable than any book ever written. But the Bible does not support some kind of leap-in-the-dark faith. Biblical faith is based on facts. God is not some vague All, or force, or some imaginary thought. Instead, God is someone who loves us more than we can comprehend and who has made himself known to us.

---

[12]Ibid., 192.

Go back and reread the section in this chapter on the Bible. Pay careful attention to the evidence and support for the Bible in prophecy, science, history, and archaeology. This is not only evidence for the Bible, but for God as well. All of this didn't just happen by accident and somehow fall into place. It is because of the existence of a living, all-knowing, all-powerful God.

Ultimately, one of the most incredible arguments for the existence of God is when He became a man in the person of Jesus Christ. The world was given all the proof necessary through fulfilled prophecy and the Resurrection.

JESUS CHRIST

Jesus is absolutely essential to Christianity. Without Him, Christianity has no substance or life. Muhammed isn't vital to the philosophy of Islam, nor is Buddha to Buddhism, but the person of Jesus Christ and His work determines everything about Christianity.

- Jesus had a virgin birth. The Bible, in Matthew and Luke, makes it clear that the Holy Spirit conceived Christ (Matthew 1:18; Luke 1:35). Mary had no involvement with a man prior to the birth of Jesus (Matthew 1:18–25).
- The man Jesus was fully God. He was not a man becoming God, but rather God coming into human flesh from the outside (John 1:1, 14; 10:30; Titus 2:13; 1 John 5:20).
- Jesus was also fully man. Because He was fully man, He can completely understand and empathize with us (Hebrews 2:16–18; Matthew 1:18; 4:2; 9:36; Luke 2:40; John 4:6; 8:40; 11:35; 19:28).
- Jesus claimed the authority of God. He said He had the power to forgive sins, raise the dead, and would come in the clouds and sit at the right hand of the Father (Mark 2:10; 14:62; John 6:39–40; 10:17–18).
- Jesus had the attributes of God. These qualities were openly displayed in Jesus for everyone to see and experience (Matthew 28:18, 20; Mark 3:10; 4:39; Luke 4:35; John 2:7–11, 25; Ephesians 1:19–21).
- Jesus is the Creator and the Sustainer. He is the divine Designer

and the one who keeps everything in the universe (John 1:3; Hebrews 1:3; Colossians 2:9).

- Jesus is timeless and eternal. He had no beginning and has no end. Jesus has always been the Son of God at some point in time (John 8:57–58).
- Jesus is the second person of the Trinity (the Son) revealed through flesh (John 1:1; Colossians 1:15–19; 1 John 5:7–8).
- Jesus is truth. He does not just tell the truth, He is the measure, the principle, and the standard for all truth (John 1:17, 14:6, 18:37).

The bottom line when you are examining any religion or belief system is to find out what they believe about Jesus. If it is anything less than what we have outlined above, you know that you are not dealing with the truth. "This is the way to find out if they have the Spirit of God: If a prophet acknowledges that Jesus Christ became a human being, that person has the Spirit of God. If a prophet does not acknowledge Jesus, that person is not from God. Such a person has the spirit of the Antichrist. You have heard that he is going to come into the world, and he is already here" (1 John 4:2–3).

THE DEATH OF JESUS

Jesus died for humanity's sin (the Atonement). Christ died in our place—He was our substitute—purchasing our freedom, making peace with God on our behalf, and satisfying the righteous demands of a holy God. His death is also called vicarious, which means "one in place of another." Isaiah 53:5 puts it this way: "But he was pierced for our transgressions, he was crushed for our iniquities" (NIV).

Because Jesus became human, He was mortal and could actually die for our sins. The death that Jesus suffered was not only humiliating, it was designed to be a death by torture.

But because He was without sin, He was the perfect sacrificial offering for our sin. Jesus was the perfect mediator between holy God and sinful people (Mark 10:45; Romans 3:25, 5:6–8; Colossians 1:20; 1 Timothy 2:5; 1 Peter 3:18, 2:24; Hebrews 4:15).

The death of Jesus Christ on the cross points out the uniqueness of Christianity. God did for us what we could not do for ourselves. He provided a way in which our sins could be forgiven and we could be brought into an intimate relationship with our Father in heaven. In other words, God made the first move. This is exactly opposite of what needs to happen in pagan religions. We do not make peace with God; it is God who makes peace with us. It isn't God who is brought back together with us, we are reunited to Him.

Wicca operates on a "do it for yourself" plan. Only Christianity offers salvation as a free gift, and this comes as a result of the unbelievable love God demonstrated for us when Jesus died on a cross to pay the penalty for our sins. Jesus' death provided redemption for us. The Bible teaches that we "were bought at a price" (1 Corinthians 6:20 NIV). The idea pictured here is that of a slave being purchased in a public slave market. Jesus has purchased us out of the slave market of sin and has set us free (1 Corinthians 7:23; Galatians 3:13).

Keep in mind that we know more about the details of the death of Jesus than we know about the death of any other one man in the entire ancient world.[13]

THE RESURRECTION

Without the resurrection, everything else about Christianity becomes meaningless, including the death of Christ. Romans 4:25 reminds us that Jesus was "delivered over to death for our sins and was raised to life for our justification" (NIV). In His death He took on all our sins, made us right with God, and in His resurrection He guaranteed us a place in heaven. The empty tomb assures us that all the things Jesus taught were true.

To fully grasp the importance of the resurrection, it would be good for us to clearly define it. The resurrection mentioned in the Bible is physical, not spiritual. In the original language of the New Testament Greek, the word used for *resurrection* is *anastasis nekrôn*. This literally means the "standing up of a corpse." Thus, *resurrection* in the Bible means "to stand up," and it always refers to the body. Author and Oxford scholar C. S. Lewis used to debate with the liberals of his day in England regarding their position that the Resurrection was only spir-

---

[13]McDowell, 211.

itual. Lewis would ask, "What position does a spirit take when it stands up?"

Just think about the promise that is ours as Christians. One day our dead bodies are going to "stand up" from the grave! When Paul writes about the resurrection in 1 Corinthians 15, he is not talking about a spiritual resurrection, because the soul never dies. The moment a body dies, the soul goes somewhere. According to 2 Corinthians 5:6–8, the minute a child of God is absent from the body, he is in the presence of the Lord. The fantastic thing about the Christian faith is that we never view death as the end. Instead, we look into eternity and see the hope that is offered through the resurrected life of Jesus Christ.

Let's look more closely at 1 Corinthians 15:3–8, where Paul writes about the proof of the resurrection and its prominence in the Gospel.

> I passed on to you what was most important and what had also been passed on to me—that Christ died for our sins, just as the Scriptures said. He was buried, and he was raised from the dead on the third day, as the Scriptures said. He was seen by Peter and then by the twelve apostles. After that, he was seen by more than five hundred of his followers at one time, most of whom are still alive, though some have died by now. Then he was seen by James and later by all the apostles. Last of all, I saw him, too, long after the others, as though I had been born at the wrong time.

Paul says that he's a communicator of the Gospel. The Gospel—"good news"—contains three essential facts: Jesus died for you and me, He was buried, and He rose again. There is no gospel apart from these facts. Notice there is nothing that we must do. Rather, it tells us what Jesus has already done for us. It's great news that Christ died and rose again, that He didn't just vanish. His tomb is empty and He is alive today. This gospel is not only great news, but it also has the power to change lives.

A few verses later in 1 Corinthians 15, Paul puts down a series of "ifs" as a demonstration of the importance of the resurrection of Jesus Christ. There was no question in Paul's mind that Christ might not have raised from the dead. Let's examine these "ifs" in light of the importance of the resurrection.

1. "For if there is no resurrection of the dead, then Christ has not been

raised either" (v. 13). The resurrection of the dead and Christ's rising are linked together. Based on His resurrection, Christ is the first and there will be more to follow—those who have placed their faith and trust in Him.

2. "And if Christ was not raised, then all our preaching is useless, and your trust in God is useless" (v. 14). Not only is it a waste of time to talk about Jesus, but so is Christianity a waste if Jesus has not risen from the dead physically. You might as well stop going to church and reading your Bible. There's no reason to do any of this if Christ had not conquered death.

3. "And we apostles would all be lying about God, for we have said that God raised Christ from the grave, but that can't be true if there is no resurrection of the dead" (v. 15). People don't die for what they know is a lie. But there've been many individuals—including teen-agers—who've died for a lie when they thought it was the truth. Just think of the tens of thousands of terrorists who have died for a "cause" because they believed in their leaders. The apostles were so certain that they had seen Jesus after He came back from the grave that they were willing to die for that truth.

4. "If there is no resurrection of the dead, then Christ has not been raised. And if Christ has not been raised, then your faith is useless and you are still under condemnation of your sins. In that case, all who have died believing in Christ have perished!" (v. 16–18). If Jesus hasn't conquered death, then we're all in big trouble. It means that we're all headed for an eternity in hell without Jesus. There's no hope of eternal life. Think of the millions upon millions of people throughout history who've died trusting Christ as their Savior. If Jesus is not alive, then every single one of them has perished.

5. "And if we have hope in Christ only for this life, we are the most miserable people in the world" (v. 19). Christianity is not just a religion for this life; it's a relationship for eternity. If Jesus has not conquered death, then we've been deceived and are the most miserable people on the planet. Instead, we celebrate because we know that Jesus is alive!

The evidence that Jesus actually died and rose from the grave confirms His uniqueness and proves that He is the Son of God. No one else in history has ever been able to predict His own resurrection and then fulfill it. The fact of the empty tomb was not the result of some scheme to make His resurrection plausible. Any attempt to refute it is confronted with mounds of evidence, beginning with Christ's documented appearances.

After His resurrection, Jesus appeared many times to different people. Taking all four gospels and the other New Testament writings into account, here is a chronological ordering of the Lord's recorded post-resurrection appearances:

- Resurrection Sunday (Easter): to Mary Magdalene (John 20:14–18); to the women coming back from the tomb with the angels' message (Matthew 28:8–10); in the afternoon to Peter (Luke 24:34; 1 Corinthians 15:5); toward evening to the disciples on the road to Emmaus (Luke 24:13–31); to all the apostles except Thomas (Luke 24:36–43; John 20:19–24).
- Eight days later: to the apostles, including Thomas (John 20:24–29).
- In Galilee: at the Lake of Tiberias to the seven (John 21:1–23); to the apostles and five hundred others on a mountain (1 Corinthians 15:6).
- At Jerusalem and Bethany (a second time): to James (1 Corinthians 15:7); to the eleven (Matthew 28:16–20; Mark 16:14–20; Luke 24:33–53; Acts 1:3–12).
- To Paul: near Damascus (Acts 9:3–6; 1 Corinthians 15:8); in the temple (Acts 22:17–21; 23:11).
- To Stephen outside Jerusalem (Acts 7:55).
- To John on the island of Patmos (Revelation 1:10–19).

Stop for just a moment. Let the evidence you have just read sink in. Jesus only appeared to His followers. For the most part His appearances were infrequent, with only four after Easter and before His ascension (return to heaven). There was nothing fantastic or farfetched in His appearances, and they were all different in nature—in the places they occurred, the length of time involved, the words spoken, and even the mood of the apostles. All Christ's appearances were bodily in nature because Jesus wanted the disciples to be sure of this fact (Luke 24:39–40; John 20:27).

It's absolutely amazing to think that so many people, on different days and in distinct situations, all had encounters with the risen Christ.

The resurrection of Christ means that God gave His approval to the claims and works of Jesus. These claims would have been sacrilegious if Jesus were not truly the Son of God. However, the Resurrection validates Jesus and His teaching. The empty tomb should assure us forever that all the things He taught were true. If Christ had not risen from the dead, then He wouldn't be alive to do all His post-resurrection work. We would not have an Advocate, Head of the church, or Intercessor. Ultimately, there'd be no living Person to live inside us and give us power (Romans 6:1–10; Galatians 2:20).

In the resurrected Christ we've got strength for today and hope for tomorrow.

Bear in mind, the religion of Christianity is not unique; it's Jesus Christ that sets it apart from all other religions. It's what you say and do with Jesus that ultimately is the key to you and your teen's eternal destiny.

WHAT ABOUT YOU?

For a moment let's talk about you and not your teen. It's extremely critical for your teen to have a personal relationship with the living God—but the same is true for you. Have you decided to become a follower of Jesus yet? To trust His Word—the Bible—over everything you are reading and hearing about spirituality? What do you think about God now?

You may not completely understand how God places the penalty for your sin on Jesus. Few of us really understand just how much we have been forgiven. But you don't need to understand everything all at once. God only asks you to believe and take the first step.

No one totally understands electricity. Scientists talk about it as a fundamental entity of all matter. They can create electrical charges and harness electricity to use. But as a scientist once said, "Electricity in its essence is quite unexplainable." Even though we can't completely understand electricity, that doesn't stop us from using it.

When you decide to become a Christian, you may not totally understand everything to start with. But as you read the Bible and allow God to teach you, your comprehension will grow. Keep in mind, this decision will be costly. It will cost you your favorite sins and your self-centered attitude to try to live your life without God. It may cost you some friends who don't understand why your life is so different. The decision to follow Jesus may even cost you your current dreams about the future, because God may have something planned for you that is totally different than you ever expected. The cost is high to accept Christ, but not anywhere near what it will cost you to reject Him.

If you're ready to start a relationship with Jesus Christ, take a few minutes right now and follow the steps listed below. It's a simple way to establish an intimate relationship with the living God. Becoming a follower of Jesus Christ is the most important decision you will ever make in life. There's nothing greater than experiencing God's love, forgiveness, and acceptance. Once you've made the decision to follow Jesus, life takes on a whole new meaning.

HOW YOU CAN EXPERIENCE A RELATIONSHIP WITH GOD[14]

1. God's Purpose: Peace and Life

God loves you and wants you to experience peace and life—satisfying and eternal.

"Therefore, since we have been made right in God's sight by faith, we have peace with God because of what Jesus Christ our Lord has done for us" (Romans 5:1).

"For God so loved the world that he gave his only Son, so that everyone who believes in him will not perish but have eternal life" (John 3:16).

So why don't most people have this peace and abundant life that God planned for us to possess?

2. The Problem: Our Separation

God created us in His own image to experience a meaningful and satisfying life. He did not make us like robots to automatically love and obey Him.

God gave us a will and the freedom of choice. We chose to disobey

---

[14]Adapted from "Steps to Peace With God," (World Wide Publications). Used with permission from the Billy Graham Evangelistic Association.

God and go our own willful way. We still make this choice today. This results in separation from God.

"For all have sinned; all fall short of God's glorious standard" (Romans 3:23).

"For the wages of sin is death, but the free gift of God is eternal life through Christ Jesus our Lord" (Romans 6:23).

Our choice results in separation from God. People have tried in many ways to bridge this gap between themselves and God. Our attempts to reach God include doing good things, religion, philosophy, and morality.

"There is a path before each person that seems right, but it ends in death" (Proverbs 14:12).

"Your sins have cut you off from God. Because of your sin, he has turned away and will not listen anymore" (Isaiah 59:2).

No bridge reaches God . . . except one.

3. God's Bridge: The Cross

Jesus Christ died on the cross and rose from the grave. He paid the penalty for our sin and bridged the gap between God and people.

"For there is only one God and one Mediator who can reconcile God and people. He is the man Christ Jesus" (1 Timothy 2:5).

"Christ also suffered when he died for our sins once for all time. He never sinned, but he died for sinners that he might bring us safely home to God. He suffered physical death, but he was raised to life in the Spirit" (1 Peter 3:18).

"But God showed his great love for us by sending Christ to die for us while we were still sinners" (Romans 5:8).

God has provided the only way, and every person must make a choice.

4. Our Response: Receive Christ

We have to trust Jesus Christ as Lord and Savior and receive Him by personal invitation.

"If you confess with your mouth that Jesus is Lord and believe in your heart that God raised him from the dead, you will be saved" (Romans 10:9).

"Look! Here I stand at the door and knock. If you hear me calling and open the door, I will come in, and we will share a meal as friends" (Revelation 3:20).

"But to all who believed him and accepted him, he gave the right to become children of God" (John 1:12).

Here's how you can start a relationship with Jesus (become a Christian):

1. Admit that you are a sinner.
2. Be willing to turn away from your sins (repent).
3. Believe that Jesus Christ died for you on the cross and rose from the grave.
4. Through prayer, invite Jesus Christ to come in and be in charge of your life through the Holy Spirit (receive Him as Lord and Savior).

Pray something like this:

> Dear Jesus,
> I know that I have sinned and need your forgiveness. I now turn from my sins to follow you. I believe that you died on the cross to take the punishment for my sins and that you came back to life after three days. I surrender my heart and life to you. I want you to be my Savior and follow you as Lord. Thank you for your love and for the gift of eternal life.
> In Jesus' name. Amen.

Have you decided to establish a relationship with Jesus? If so, you've made the most important decision of your life! If you have sincerely accepted Jesus, then you can trust Him. Check out what the Bible says in Romans 10:13 (NIV): "Everyone who calls on the name of the Lord will be saved."

When we surrender our lives to Jesus, we become brand-new people. Check out the promise in 2 Corinthians 5:17. "What this means is that those who become Christians become new persons. They are not the same anymore, for the old life is gone. A new life has begun!" The Holy Spirit gives us new life and we're not the same anymore. We are not rehabilitated or reeducated. Instead, we are new creations living in vital union with Jesus (see Colossians 2:6–7). A supernatural conversion takes place the moment we accept Christ. We don't just change some stuff in our life, we start a new life under a new Master.

This is something that Wicca does not offer. But there's a catch: In order to get this new life, you have to surrender the old one. You must give up control, which is opposite to the teachings of Wicca. And this is opposite of what our culture says. *Surrender* is a negative word, because we are told the way to freedom and becoming an individual is staying in charge. That's why Wicca is so popular today—because people not only make their own deities, they are the god of their own life.

But God is the One who made you and knows what is best for you. The only way we can experience real purpose in our life, as well as wisdom for the tough stuff we face, is by surrendering our lives to Jesus.

This relationship that you have established is one that cannot be broken or terminated. Jesus promises to never let you down and never give you up (Hebrews 13:5). This is the core of Christianity. It's not a religion; it's God revealing himself to us, rescuing us from our sin, and making it possible for us to experience a relationship with Him.

And just like you would do in any other relationship, remember to stay in touch with your new best friend. You can do this in a couple of ways. Start by reading the letters Jesus has already given you telling about who He is, how He can help you, how to live your life, and most of all how much He loves you. All this and much more is found in the Bible. Take time each day to read and study a portion of it. And just like you might instant-message a friend on the Internet, you can send an instant message to God through prayer. You can pray anytime, anyplace, and you don't even have to be online!

Make sure you get plugged in to a church where they teach about Jesus, from the Bible, and where you can worship and develop friendships with other Christians. Remember to tell others what Jesus has done for you, because they can experience the same thing. And look for ways to serve God by helping others in need in the world.

You may feel totally different now or you may not. The most important thing is that you now know how you can start a relationship with the living God, and you will have the rest of eternity to develop and experience it!

And by the way, if you did say a prayer to place your faith and trust in Jesus Christ, please let me know by using the contact information in the back of this book. This is just the beginning of a great new life with Jesus. I want to pray for you and send you some things to help you get started growing in this new relationship with God.

As I said earlier in this chapter, having a personal relationship with God is also extremely critical for your teen. If you've just accepted Christ, tell your teen. This may mean stepping out of your comfort zone, but it's important that your son or daughter hear about the choice that you've made. This will give you a better foundation from which to talk with them about the need they have to accept Jesus. You may even want to use the information in this chapter to talk with them about the Bible, God, and Jesus. And you can even use the steps and prayer mentioned earlier to introduce them to Jesus.

ONE FINAL THOUGHT

The most important question you and your teen will ever answer is: "Who is Jesus?" I've tried to give as much information as possible for you to be able to answer this question. Take your time. Give very careful and thoughtful attention to what we've discussed in this book. Don't take my word for it—examine the facts. Check out the evidence for yourself.

Wiccan author Scott Cunningham passed from this life after a long illness. If it were possible to speak with him today, I wonder what he would say to us about spirituality. I question whether or not he would change the dedication in one of his books that reads: "This book is dedicated to the forces that watch over and guide us—however we may envision or name them." What would Scott say about God now?

Jesus made the initial choice—to love and to die for us, and to invite us to live with Him forever. We must make the next choice—to accept or reject His offer. Without His choice, we would have no choice to make. Now it's up to you—whose word are you going to trust?

CHAPTER 11:

PARENTING A DIGITAL GENERATION

HAVE YOU EVER FELT like screaming, "Help! I'm the parent of a teenager"? Or maybe you've been looking for a place where you can resign as a parent? Trust me, you're not alone.

I co-host a live call-in radio show for teens every Saturday night called *Life on the Edge—Live!* Without fail, every week my co-host, Susie Shellenberger, and I have to remind our audience that "this is teen talk radio—adults, keep your hands away from the phone and keep the lines open for our teen listeners." We've even had parents coaching their kids what questions to ask once we put them on the air.

Life is confusing and complex for today's teens, as well as for their parents and grandparents. There is a battle raging in the minds and emotions of our kids. So much is coming at them from so many different directions. They have open, interested minds and soft hearts. Moreover, they are individuals with a tremendous spiritual hunger, seeking help and hope to navigate through the enticements of contemporary culture like witchcraft.

It's not easy being a mom or dad today—especially if you're a single parent. And everyone knows that parenting is a hazardous business. There are no money-back guarantees that everything will turn out well for our kids. However, God does give us a promise in Proverbs 22:6:

"Teach your children to choose the right path, and when they are older, they will remain upon it." God has given each of us a unique set of talents and abilities. Part of our responsibility as parents is to discern the individual strengths of our children and help them to develop these capabilities. Part of this process is to train them how to choose the right path in life. The main objective is to help our kids be who they were created to be.

The key to confident parenting in confusing times is based on taking God's Word seriously and applying it to every dimension of life—including parenting. It's practical, timely, and relevant to all the issues of life, including how to protect our teens against today's witchcraft.

WHAT'S YOUR APPROACH TO COMMUNICATING WITH YOUR TEEN?

One of the biggest and most common problems families face today is the lack of healthy communication. It's an ever-increasing cause of frustration among teens and parents alike. Communication can simply be defined as the act of sharing or exchanging information. Stop and think about that definition for a minute.

- When was the last time you shared or exchanged ideas with your teen?
- How much time did you spend interacting with him or her?
- Is the exchange of information with your son or daughter one-sided?

Healthy, loving communication is crucial when it comes to parenting a digital generation.

Dr. Larry Richards has provided a helpful explanation of parent–child communication. Drawing from the work of Ross Snyder, Richards characterizes four levels of parental response and communication through the following illustration.

A child in a boat is headed for certain disaster. He obviously made a bad decision upstream. His parent will respond in one of four ways.

1. The *advice giver* is far removed from the emotional crisis. He hollers, "Row harder! Why did you get into the water in the first place? What a stupid kid! I told you not to do it. Didn't

you read the warning signs?"

2. The *reassurer* is closer to the situation and responds, "You were a good kid. Your mother and I love you. Of the last three people who went over the falls, two survived. Good luck!"

3. The *understander* steps into the water and says, "Hey, the current is very strong here. You really are in trouble, aren't you? Let me see if I can get you some help."

4. The *self-revealer* gets into the boat with the child and immediately starts paddling to safety.

Here's another example that hits a little closer to home; it's one you've probably experienced. Suppose your teen comes home from school and he's obviously upset. It's written all over his face and you see it in his body language. You ask him what's wrong, and he tells you that his girlfriend has dumped him. How would you respond?

If you're an advice-giver you might say something like, "I never did like that girl anyway. What'd you do to make her dump you? Next time be more careful about choosing your friends. I think what you need to do is . . ."

If you're a reassurer you will probably wrap your arms around him and say, "You know that I love you. You're a good kid, and I know you'll survive this crisis. You'll find another friend."

If you're an understander, you might respond, "Hey, that hurts, doesn't it? Can we sit down and talk about it? Tell me everything that happened."

However, if you're a self-revealer, you'll give him a hug and sit quietly with him for a moment reflecting on a time you were dumped or rejected. Then you may respond, "Two years ago my best friend turned his back on me. I trusted him as much as I trusted anyone. It was one of the most painful experiences of my life. I sense you're going through the same thing as I did."

I informally surveyed hundreds of teenagers to find out how their parents respond to similar situations. Ninety-five percent identified their parents as advice-givers. Five percent said their parents were reassurers. Not one teenager identified their parents as an understander or self-revealer. Don't misunderstand, I'm not saying that you don't need to give advice and offer reassurance to your teen from time to time. And obviously there's no one particular response that's appropriate in every situation. But a serious communication problem exists when teens report that their parents respond almost exclusively with advice-giving and reassurance.

When your son or daughter is hurt or in trouble, he or she needs a self-revealer to "get into the boat" with them. If you don't learn to integrate and apply this communication style, your teen may eventually gravitate toward even more damaging choices. It should be our objective to be the kind of parent a son or daughter can feel comfortable coming to and confiding in. If our kids know that we will respond to them with love, trust, and respect—no matter what they tell us—they'll open up like flowers in the warm sun. Make a commitment to doing all you can to establish healthy communication with your teen. Remember, it's up to you as the parent to ensure that this happens.

DOES YOUR PARENTING STYLE NEED SOME IMPROVEMENT?

As parents, we must decide to be actively involved in every dimension of our children's lives. The more involved we become in the lives of our kids, the more time we must sacrifice. But remember, it will always cost you something—you're either going to pay now or later. If you wait until later, it's always more expensive.

When you start getting more involved in the life of your kids, you'll learn what their likes and dislikes are, and you'll also learn to appreciate them. As our kids get older, they get busier, but that should not preclude our being involved in their lives. Do you enjoy spending time with your kids and doing things that interest them? Have you developed a mutual interest in activities that you can do together?

Spend time building relationships with your teens. It's important to healthy communication, and the other benefits are awesome as well!

Now let's take a look at some practical ideas for parenting a digital generation. These ideas are foundational for understanding your kids and building healthy relationships with them. Be careful not to just glance through them. Simply doing a basic review of things isn't enough. The real issue is whether you're actually doing these things.

1. Get in Touch With Your Kids

All too frequently I find that parents know more about their ancestral family tree than they do about the current activities of their teens.

That's why an important element of parenting is understanding the likes, dislikes, and lifestyles of our kids. This can only happen when a conscious effort is made to invade their world and counter their culture. Without this hands-on knowledge, it's tough to earn the right to be heard or the respect of your teens.

As a parent you can attempt to enforce the right to be heard, but it's not nearly as effective as earning it. In 1 Corinthians 9:22 we find a truth that can be applied for this very element of parenting. "When I am with those who are oppressed, I share their oppression so that I might bring them to Christ. Yes, I try to find common ground with everyone so that I might bring them to Christ." The apostle Paul gives some important thoughts for parenting: Establish common ground with your teen and avoid a know-it-all attitude. Learn from your teen about their world, letting them know you accept them for who they are. Also, be sensitive to their needs and concerns. Most importantly, look for opportunities to live out and share your faith with your kids.

This takes time. How much time do you spend with your kids? When was the last time you took your son or daughter on a date? It doesn't have to be expensive. It could be something as simple as taking them out for a soft drink. Make sure you try to do something they want to do. The objective is to spend some quality time interacting with them.

2. Learn to Listen

Have you noticed what poor listeners we have become in our culture? If it's frustrating for us as adults, just imagine how frustrating it is for teens. I like what it says in Proverbs 18:13 about listening—especially in light of parenting a teenager. "What a shame, what folly, to give advice before listening to the facts!" Sometimes it's easy to advise or correct your teen in a given situation before you've really heard—with careful attention—what he or she is trying to say. This takes time and effort, but it beats becoming like the person who is always saying, "Don't confuse me with the facts!"

Kids today need their parents to do more than just hear them out. They need moms and dads who will carefully listen to them. *Webster's* dictionary defines listening as "to hear with thoughtful attention." Do you really listen to your kids? How about your spouse? James 1:19

offers this additional advice in regard to listening: "Dear friends, be quick to listen, slow to speak, and slow to get angry." When it comes to parenting, put a mental stopwatch on your conversations and keep track of how much you talk and how much you listen. Listening demonstrates to our kids that we really do care and think that what they have to say is important. Learning to listen can greatly improve parent–teen relationships.

3. Work at Understanding

Do you really comprehend the challenges your teens are facing in their world today? Forty percent of kids surveyed say that their views are either ignored or bypassed by parents. Consequently, they conclude that their parents don't really care about them or their opinions. Our ability to grasp their outlook about different issues in life enables us to better demonstrate our care and concern for them, as well as to provide proper guidance for tackling the issues of life. Learning to understand them is foundational to building positive relationships with your teens.

At the core of understanding are two important concepts. First, parents must become thoroughly familiar with the character, personality, and disposition of each child. Second, they must work at putting themselves in the position of their son or daughter to gain more insight about the world in which they live. When speaking to parents, I often comment, "I know you're aware that we live in the twenty-first century, but do you realize what that means in relating to your kids?"

Things are remarkably different today than when we grew up. Certainly there are similar problems, as with previous generations—drug and alcohol abuse, premarital sex, and rebellion, to name a few. However, the problems teens are facing today are more complex, and the intensity is far greater than for any previous generation. That's why it's important for parents to work harder at understanding the world of their young person. A lot of the strain between parents and teens today could be reduced through better communication and understanding. It's been said, "Home is not where you live but where they understand you."

Proverbs 11:12 reminds us "a person with good sense remains silent." How many times have you said something you regretted right after the words rolled past your lips? Imagine how different family life might be if parents worked harder at understanding their kids' perspective before talking. Earlier in this chapter we talked about the importance of earning the right to be heard. Gaining favor through understanding can help us navigate through a multitude of teenage issues.

4. Be a Source of Encouragement

Let's be honest. We all need encouragement, and this is especially true of teenagers today. Our world's not a very encouraging place to live. Confusion, pain, and disillusionment enshroud this generation. That's why it is so important for our homes to be places of hope and help. Kids need a safe refuge where they're sure someone cares and wants the best for them.

Encouragement is an important principle woven throughout the New Testament. Look at 1 Thessalonians 5:11: "So encourage each other and build each other up, just as you are already doing." Life is a long-distance marathon. There are times when your feet ache, your throat burns, and your whole body cries out for you to stop. This is when you need to have supporters, people who believe in you. Their encouragement helps to push you along and motivates you to hang in there. This is especially true for parents and their teenagers. A word of encouragement said at just the right time can be the difference between continuing to run the race of life and collapsing along the way. Be sensitive to the need for encouragement that your teens may have; offer supportive words and demonstrate them by your actions.

5. Give Them Boundaries

I'll never forget a conversation I had with a teenage guy about boundaries. "Russo, I wish my parents would give me a curfew. I want them to tell me what time to be home. Instead, they tell me to come home whenever." Kids want boundaries. They test their parents to see how far they can go—what they can get away with. Boundaries say, "I care about you." And they give kids a sense of security, which is one of three core needs kids have. The other two are acceptance and significance. All three together make up one's identity. Struggling with identity is a huge issue with teens today. But one of the main reasons kids are struggling with identity is because their parents are still dealing with the same issue.

In several places in the Old Testament we read about God setting up and establishing boundaries for His people. Why? They needed protection, guidance, and security, among other things. Teens need the same thing today from their parents. Remember who the parent is— you! They may kick and scream at first, and they may never thank you, but they need realistic and fair boundaries to survive.

6. Choose Your Battles

One of the toughest things you may do as the parent of a teenager is learn how to choose your battles. This does not mean you compromise or ignore behavior, but you look at the big picture. Put another way: Do you want to win the battle or the war? It will not be easy, but you may find yourself not confronting your son or daughter on a particular issue because you see the bigger picture and realize that there's more to the problem than meets the eye. You need God's wisdom in order to be capable of doing this.

I like the way Solomon put it centuries ago. "Since a dull ax requires great strength, sharpen the blade. That's the value of wisdom; it helps you succeed" (Ecclesiastes 10:10). When you find yourself having to choose your battles with your teenager, turn to God and His Word for wisdom.

7. Love Them Genuinely

Everyone knows how important love is, but we usually think of it as a feeling. In reality, genuine love is a choice and an action. First Corinthians 13:4–7 puts it this way: "Love is patient and kind. Love is not jealous or boastful or proud or rude. Love does not demand its own way. Love is not irritable, and it keeps no record of when it has been wronged. It is never glad about injustice but rejoices whenever the truth wins out. Love never gives up, never loses faith, is always hopeful, and endures through every circumstance."

These verses offer a great checklist to examine the kind of love parents should demonstrate to their teens. Kids need this kind of love if they're going to survive in a digital world and face things like Wicca. However, the kind of love the Bible is talking about is not humanly possible without help. God is the source of our love; He loved us enough to sacrifice His only Son for us, taking the punishment for our sins. Jesus is the ultimate example of what it means to love. Everything He did in His life and His death was a demonstration of God's love for us. Once we've experienced God's love, His Spirit gives us the power to love others. Loving others God's way always involves a choice and an action.

THE BIG "H" IN PARENTING

When I first began traveling and speaking, one of the most requested topics I was asked to address was on contemporary music. My primary audience was teenagers for a presentation that I had titled "How Is Rock Music Changing Your Life?" Having spent a number of years in the music industry as a professional drummer, I felt like I could approach the subject with more than just an average platform of credibility.

One particular weekend I was speaking at a series of meetings at a church in northern California, including a Sunday afternoon session for teens on music. A couple with a southern twang in their voices approached me at the end of the Sunday morning service. "Reverend Russo, we're mighty grateful that y'all are addressing the evils of that rock music with the young people this afternoon, here in the Lord's house." They went on to voice all their concerns about rock music, including the lifestyle of musicians, the beat and lyrical content. After thanking them for their encouragement, I thought I'd have some fun. "By the way, folks, what kind of music do you listen to?" I asked.

They both stood up straight and tall, shoulders pushed back, and responded, "Well, we listen to American music. You know—we like to call it God's music." "And what kind of music might that be?" I posed. "Country western, of course," they said. It was hard to keep myself from laughing. Here they stood criticizing various elements of rock music yet were seemingly oblivious to some of the very same elements contained in country music. By the way, sometimes I even wonder if country western is worse than rock music—because you can actually understand most of the lyrics!

Have you noticed how easy it is to slip into hypocrisy—especially in regard to parenting? For example: We hammer our kids relentlessly when it comes to the contemporary music they listen to or the Web sites they go to, yet we fail to use the same standards for selecting our music or the movies that we watch. How many parents shred their teen's music, then turn right around and watch TV shows that are no more wholesome? Too many times I've heard the lame excuse, "Well, I'm an adult." I've not found any biblical basis for an adult being exempt from God's command to maintain purity of mind.

Nothing will undermine your ability to be an effective parent more quickly than hypocrisy. And don't deceive yourself into believing that you can get away with feigning to be what you are not in front of your kids. They can spot a phony a mile away. Adolescents are generally the quickest to discern hypocrisy. Kids today are searching for role models who are real and genuine—people who live life with integrity and consistency. And this search begins at home with Mom and Dad.

Jesus speaks strongly against being a hypocrite in the book of Matthew. "And why worry about a speck in your friend's eye when you have a log in your own? How can you think of saying, 'Friend, let me help you get rid of that speck in your eye,' when you can't see past the log in your own eye? Hypocrite! First get rid of the log from your own eye; then perhaps you will see well enough to deal with the speck in your friend's eye" (7:3–5). The principle here for living is to carefully examine our own lives first before judging or criticizing others—including our kids.

Unfortunately, sometimes the traits that bother us in our teens are often the habits we dislike in ourselves. Do you find it easy to magnify your kids' faults while ignoring your own? Or how about demanding your kids practice certain disciplines—spiritual or otherwise—that you don't exercise consistently in your own? Maybe it's time for an attitude adjustment when it comes to the Big H.

How far does your hypocrisy actually extend? Let's examine some of the more common problem areas when it comes to parenting and hypocrisy:

1. *Manners*: Do you insist on your kids saying "please" and "thank you" but fail to do so yourself? What about reminding them to keep their arms off the table when eating, but it's okay for you to do it?

2. *Church*: Do you tell your kids how important it is for them to be involved in church, yet you skip out whenever possible, util-

izing weak excuses and rationalizations?

3. *Devotions*: Do you badger your kids about the importance of having daily time alone with God, but you fail to practice this important spiritual discipline in your own life?

4. *Language*: Do you consistently remind your kids that they should always tell the truth, and at times you even punish them for lying, yet they hear you tell half-truths and lies over and over again? Do you issue warnings to your kids that their use of foul language will result in some form of discipline, yet you find yourself utilizing some pretty colorful language with them or other adults?

5. *Music, Movies, and the Internet*: Do you tell your kids to be more selective in the music they listen to or the movies they watch, yet you don't think twice about some of the entertainment garbage you allow into your mind? Has the Internet become a source of stress in your family as you attempt to establish guidelines for where your kids can and cannot go on the Web, but your own cyberspace surfing has no limits?

Obviously, we have only scratched the surface of hypocritical traps that parents find themselves falling into with their teens. In the struggle against hypocrisy, remember a couple of things. First, our kids watch us like hawks to see if we are living consistently. Second, the heart of this issue is not perfection. That's not what God expects from us. However, if this is a struggle in your life, God does expect us to rely upon His help and power to resist hypocrisy.

Maybe it's time for you to get real with yourself, your teens, and with God. Start by being honest with your kids about your desire to live a life of integrity. Then with God's help, strive to be more consistent in adhering to biblical standards and disciplines in your own life that you had previously been emphasizing to your kids. Finally, find someone to be accountable to—either your spouse or a friend.

Hypocrisy is a dangerous game of pretense for you and your teens. It's a form of deception that undermines the trust that is necessary for solid parent–teen relationships. Plus, it sends the wrong message to our kids that it's okay to live by the philosophy, "Do as I say, not as I do." Parenting is tough enough today without adding hypocrisy to the mix. Stop being a false witness to yourself. And remember, there's tremendous freedom and power in the truth—for you and your kids.

THE BOTTOM LINE

Parenting is never easy. It takes time, energy, and effort. In the last twenty years we've seen increased spending on education and social welfare, parents who are better educated, families that are smaller, and yet our children are at greater risk than ever before. Why? A major contributing factor is a generation of parents who are unwilling to spend time building values into the lives of their children. There's no substitute for sharing our lives with our kids. A simple way to stay in touch with your kids and spend time with them is to try and have one meal per day as a family. Sit together around the table and keep the TV off. Mealtime can be a great opportunity to connect as a family and to find out about each member's activities for the day. The concept of having a meal together may be new to your family, but it is definitely worth making a priority in your home.

Ultimately, if we want our teens to survive in this digital culture, we must not only spend time building values into their lives, we must also help them develop a vital, personal relationship with Jesus Christ. He is our strength, hope, and peace in a confused world that has lost its way. But we can't help our kids secure something we don't have ourselves. Make sure you've settled things with Jesus first, and then you can better help your teenage son or daughter.

CHAPTER 12:

WHEN YOUR TEEN IS INTO WICCA

IT CAUGHT YOUR ATTENTION when you least expected it. Your son was taking some things out of his backpack and you noticed a copy of Scott Cunningham's book *Wicca: A Guide for the Solitary Practitioner*. What do you do?

Amanda didn't realize how enticing witchcraft could be: "I saw the movie *The Craft* and was instantly hooked." She grew up in a Christian home and knew it was wrong, but she wanted to know more about it. Amanda started studying Wicca and became involved for several months. She began doubting God and questioned her relationship with Him. Amanda still went to church every Sunday, but basically zoned out and wasn't paying attention. "My life basically just went down the drain." At a weekend retreat with her church youth group, she realized what was happening to her and came back to God. When Amanda got home she threw away everything she owned that had to do with Wicca. "When I think how far I separated myself from God, I get goose bumps. It's scary to be away from His love."

Jake was a Wiccan for two years, but with the help of a friend and a Bible study he attended, he found Christ. "I realized that Wicca was not fulfilling my spiritual needs. I was not sure how to break away and go to the God who loves me." But a friend helped him see the love and benefits that living with Jesus could give.

Do you have a son or daughter into witchcraft? What can we do to help those we love who are involved in a self-styled religion that denies Jesus is God? Before we talk about what we can do, let me remind you about a few things that you should *not* do.

The initial reaction is usually to deny that your child would even be involved in witchcraft. You can deny it all you want, but that won't change the situation. Because your son or daughter may be involved in witchcraft does not necessarily mean that you're a failure as a parent, but it does mean that you need to take action.

When reality sets in, you panic, yell a little, and throw away any witchcraft materials that your son or daughter may have collected. Don't give in to this temptation—as upset as you may be. Calm down and get some perspective before you do anything. You don't want to say or do something you'll regret later, or magnify the problem that already exists. Take some time to pray and ask God for insight into the situation.

A lot of teens today are living in spiritual darkness. The devil has done a masterful job at getting them to believe his lies. "Satan, the god of this evil world, has blinded the minds of those who don't believe, so they are unable to see the glorious light of the Good News that is shining upon them. They don't understand the message we preach about the glory of Christ, who is the exact likeness of God" (2 Corinthians 4:4).

Be careful that you don't underestimate the deceptive power of witchcraft—even if your teen claims to be a follower of Jesus. Seventeen-year-old Sara calls herself a hardcore Christian and says she's extremely active in her church and youth group. But when it comes to Wicca, she's bought the lie. "My attitude toward Wicca is that it really doesn't mean anything. It is totally fake. I don't think it is good, but it is not bad either. It really doesn't do anything."

Those involved in Wicca and witchcraft have bought the lie of religion that says you can get to heaven—or however you describe life after death—through your own efforts and in your own way. Let's face it: That's an easy trap to fall into. We're so used to earning things by working for them. Even as little children we are taught that if we do a certain thing we will be rewarded. We then want to carry this over to religion. It's hard to accept the fact that something as significant as eternal life is a free gift from God. Satan complicates matters with his lies, and unfortunately many people believe him. You and I have the privilege of rescuing our children who have become spiritual hostages of the enemy (2 Timothy 2:26).

WARNING SIGNS

After reading this chapter you may be thinking, *My teen is a good kid. He's not into stuff like Satanism, the occult, or drugs.* Hopefully you're right. But if he were dabbling in the occult, witchcraft, or drugs, would you know it? Remember: Satan is a deceiver. If he is seducing your teen in these areas, he doesn't want your son or you to know about it.

I share with you now some of the symptoms and warning signs of possible involvement in Satanism, the occult, witchcraft, and drugs. If your teen exhibits any of the following behaviors or possessions, don't jump to conclusions too quickly, or react too slowly, to the potential danger. Be prayerful, cautious, concerned, and ready to act.

A teen's involvement in occultic activities usually involves one or more of the following:

1. *Withdrawal from routine activities*—the normal everyday stuff. Beware of unusual seclusion or secrecy by your teen.
2. *Obsession with death and suicide.* Many who practice Wicca believe in reincarnation. Pay attention to the music your teen is listening to and the DVDs they are watching—and anything else they're feeding their mind. Also watch for a fascination or the possession of knives, as they can be used in satanic rituals or sacrifices. But be careful. There's a fine line to balance here between oversight/investigation and respecting their privacy. The first step is to just pay attention to what you can see without having to look or dig very far in their rooms or cars. If casual observations raise questions and concerns, then investigate further. You want not only to protect your teens, but to respect them as well. No one wants to feel like someone else is constantly rifling through their possessions with no valid reason. The best-case scenario is to develop open communication with them.
3. *Fixation with Wiccan symbols and runes.* These symbols can be

found in and on a variety of items, including a Book of Shadows and correspondence. Runes are symbols that when drawn, painted, traced, carved, or visualized are believed to release specific energies.[1] Many of these symbols are explained in Appendix E.

4. *Possession of Wiccan, pagan, and shamanistic publications.* These could be in the form of books, newsletters, magazines, and tabloids. Topics and content could include poetry, spells, songs, rituals, herb craft, artwork, etc.

5. *Excessive fears or anxiety.* If your teen exhibits unusual preoccupation and paranoia about current events in the world situation, at school, or at home, then you have a reason to be concerned.

6. *Cuts, scratches, burns, and tattoos.* Look for scars or tattoos in the shape of occultic symbols on hidden parts of the body. In the extreme situation, watch for missing fingers and toes. Any unusual health problems should be thoroughly investigated.

7. *Religious artifacts and bells.* Watch for articles that are used in occultic rituals, such as chalices, goblets, bells, and gongs. Bells and gongs are used to purify the air and dismiss the demons at the conclusion of the ceremony.

8. *Altars.* They can be simple or extremely elaborate, and located in a bedroom closet, basement, garage, or attic. Usually they are placed within a witch's circle, which is considered sacred space. They can have candles, incense, photographs, or even personal effects on them. It all depends on the function of the magick to be performed.

Keep in mind that just because you observe one or more of these signs in your teen's life, it does not mean that they are involved in Wicca. But it could mean that they are facing some tough issues and need some help.

PRACTICAL TIPS

To rescue someone from Wicca or another form of spiritual darkness, we must first fully understand the level of commitment and preparation that must be in place in our own lives. Like all good soldiers,

---

[1]Cunningham, 177.

we must be prepared for battle. Let's look at some practical things we need to remember as we try to help a teen who's involved in witchcraft.

1. Approach them gradually. You need to be aware of what they believe spiritually and try to understand where they're coming from. Be patient and take them one step at a time closer to an understanding of what it really means to have a relationship with Jesus.
2. Try to find out what unmet need seems to be met in Wicca. That can be a starting point for telling them how Jesus has met this need in your own life—or someone else you know—and how He can do the same for them.
3. Be very sensitive to their perspective. Don't make fun of their involvement in Wicca, as illogical as it may seem. This will only cause them to avoid discussing their "religion" with you. Listen to them very carefully.
4. Try to find common ground. Ask questions about the way they personally practice witchcraft to see what might be similar to Christianity. Remember, most Wiccans are solitary practitioners. Establishing common ground can be a great starting point for discussion. It could be things like
   • living a moral life
   • environmental issues
   • finding personal peace
   • the importance of self-discipline
   • concern for gender equality
   • prayer and meditation
   • what God is like
   • the source of power
5. Highlight the differences between Wicca and Christianity. Most people involved in Wicca have never really heard the truth about what Christians believe and what the Bible teaches. Check out the Quick Reference Comparison Guide in Appendix A for some help.
6. Clarify terms and definitions. Familiarize yourself with Wiccan and witchcraft terms. Check out the glossary of terms in Appendix C. But remember, you don't need to expose yourself to witchcraft to effectively help lead someone out of it.
7. Show by example your trust in God alone. Help your teen see

that the only source of security, acceptance, and significance in this world is found in a relationship with Jesus Christ.

8. Be open about your faith in a personal God, not some "force," god and goddess, or self-made deity. Emphasize the benefits of a relationship with a personal God, with things like

- He is able to love us,
- He can hear and answer our prayers,
- He can sympathize with our pain.

   And don't forget that it's also important for you to share how you define God.

9. Clearly explain the issue of sin and the opportunity we have for forgiveness. No other religion offers complete and total forgiveness for sin like Christianity. Only Jesus gave His life for ours and offers eternal life. Wicca offers nothing like this.

10. Use the Bible strategically to explain and support what you believe. Make sure that personal study of the Bible is a priority in your own life. Unfortunately, most Christians are not equipped to respond biblically when talking with those involved in Wicca and witchcraft. Make sure you can share why you believe the Bible is God's Word, and be prepared with evidence you have to support that it's true.

   We're involved in a battle for truth, not power. We must help our teens to accept God's truth in their lives and stop believing the lies that Satan has fed their minds. Satan's only power is in his deceptive lies. The light of God's truth shatters the lies of the devil and sets us free to be the people God designed us to be.

11. Consistently pray for and with your children.

12. Focus on Jesus. It all comes down to who you believe Jesus is; that's why it's important to point to Him as much as possible. Help your teen see that He is more than a prophet, a good teacher, or just a man. He is God. And remember to help your teen understand that

- the All and Jesus both can't be right;
- the god/goddess and Jesus both can't be right;
- self-made deities and Jesus all can't be right.

   Encourage your teens to read the New Testament books of Mark and John, so they learn more about the life and work of Jesus. Jesus is unique; there is no other religious leader like Him—never has been and never will be. If we have a relationship with Jesus, we have been given the awesome responsibility to tell others the "good news" of salvation through Him. It is singularly the most important information in history, because it offers the truth of the only door to heaven and fulfillment here on earth. Jesus said, "I am the way, the truth and the life. No one can come to the Father except through me" (John 14:6).

Remember your ultimate goal is for your teen to be freed from the spiritual darkness of Wicca and place their faith and trust in Jesus. But this may take some time. Be patient and never lose sight of your goal. Ask questions about their beliefs, and respond in a caring way. Don't forget the unseen spiritual battle mentioned in Ephesians 6 that we are all involved in. We battle a fierce enemy, but one who was critically wounded when Jesus died on the cross.

And don't forget, God cares about our teens even more than we do. So don't give up hope!

CHILDREN ARE SPECIAL TO GOD

Parents need to become more aware of just how much children mean to God. They have a God-given responsibility not only to protect children from physical abuse, but from spiritual corruption as well. Jesus gives a stern warning in Luke 17:2–3 for those who abuse or lead astray little ones: "It would be better to be thrown into the sea with a millstone hung around your neck than to cause one of these little ones to fall into sin. So watch yourselves!"

It's also important for us to remember that throughout history, God has used young people to change the course of history. They are the most precious natural resource that we have. Nothing is more valuable to us than our children, and we must do all we can to protect them and help guide them through the land mines of life.

I owe my life to a teenager. And that's why I'm so committed to helping them be all that God designed them to be. Robbie was taking drum lessons from me while I was still in the music industry. Each week during his lesson he would tell me about his best friend. He told me how he shared everything with this friend, but he never told me his best friend's name. I actually started to become envious of Robbie and this relationship he had with his best friend, because I didn't have a friend like he did. One day before the lesson started, I finally asked Robbie what his best friend's name was. His response just about knocked me over. "Jesus!" Robbie said. "And He can be your best friend, too." It wasn't long after that I met Robbie's aunt and uncle, Billy and Danielle, who were Christians and entertainers in Hollywood, and they helped me put my faith and trust in Jesus.

As a result of one teenager's courage to tell me about his "best friend," people across the United States and in twenty-four foreign countries have heard the message of God's love through our ministry.

God used a teenager in my life, and He wants to work through your teen to help others. As you become aware of the spiritual condition of your children, ask God how He wants to use you to help them find answers in a relationship with Jesus. He said, "You are the light of the world—like a city on a mountain, glowing in the night for all to see. Don't hide your light under a basket! Instead, put it on a stand and let it shine for all" (Matthew 5:14–15).

One person really can make a difference in the world!

CONCLUSION: PROTECTING YOUR TEEN

AS A TEENAGER, Sean Sellers was involved in Satanism and the occult. This involvement proved to be deadly, as he ended up convicted of murdering his parents. Sean made an astonishing statement about his involvement in the darkness. He claimed that if he had had a close family relationship, he might not have gotten into the occult and Satan worship.

Obviously, Sean is not an authority on family matters, but he certainly gives us something to think about when considering how to protect our teens from today's witchcraft. The primary means to guard our teens from dabbling with the spiritual fire is to flood their lives with the light of a Christ-centered family relationship. Let's look at specific ways you can accomplish this in your home.

1. Show your teens the way to Jesus.

The first and most important step in protecting your teens from the influence of witchcraft and the occult is to help them establish a personal relationship with Jesus Christ. Don't just assume they're following

Jesus because they attend church. Remember, God has no grand-children. Your teens must make their own personal commitment to place their faith and trust in Jesus. And who better to help them with this than their mom or dad?

Here are some important guidelines to remember in this process:

- Pray regularly for them to establish a relationship with Christ. As much as you may want to, you can't force or argue them into following Jesus. Nevertheless, you can pray and allow the Holy Spirit to prepare their hearts to be open to spiritual truth. The very top of your prayer list should be to see your teens put their trust in Christ.

- Frequently share what God is doing in your life. Talk with them about spiritual truths you have learned and answers to prayer you have received.

- Communicate stories and relate life experiences to the Bible. Teens can often better understand concepts when they are presented through stories. Make use of personal stories about how you came to know God as well as biblical stories about individuals who were challenged to give their lives to Christ. For example: Jesus talks with Nicodemus (John 3); Jesus and the Samaritan woman (John 4); Philip and the Ethiopian (Acts 8).

- Convey a simple Gospel presentation. At some point in time you need to clearly and lovingly share with your teens how they can receive Christ. There are quite a few good tracts and booklets available to help you accomplish this. You can also go back to chapter 10, "Fact, Fiction, or Feeling," and review the steps in how to establish a personal relationship with God. Make sure to stress God's forgiveness and unconditional love.

    As you talk with your teens, make sure you use common language they can understand. Avoid speaking "Christianese." Stay away from using Christian jargon like "saved," "redeemed," "sanctified," and "repent." Share the truth of the Gospel simply and clearly.

- Give a clear invitation. Don't try to manipulate—allow the Spirit of God to work. However, after some discussion and answering questions, at some point you need to simply ask them, "Are you ready to put your faith and trust in Jesus Christ right now?" If they answer "yes," you can use the prayer in chapter 10 as a guide to help them.

- If you have the privilege of being the one to lead them to Christ, review the decision with them. You want to help them as much as possible to understand what has just happened. Here are some sample questions:
  - What did you just do?
  - What did Jesus do when you opened your heart to Him (see Revelation 3:20)?
  - What did you become when you put your faith and trust in Jesus (see John 1:12)?
  - Where is Jesus right now?

2. Cultivate a spiritually healthy family.

Our teens need to understand that Jesus is always with us (individually and as a family) and wants to be intimately involved in our day-to-day lives. A spiritually healthy family is one where Jesus is at the center—at the very core. Just as the planets revolve around the sun, so should our families revolve around Jesus.

You can begin by making sure that this is in fact happening in your personal lives as parents first. Remember, more is caught than taught. You need to model this concept. Has Jesus consumed your life? Have you allowed Him to invade every aspect of your life—from work to recreation? Do your teens see you depending upon Jesus in every circumstance? Do they observe you reading the Bible? Do they hear you talking about God answering your prayers?

Your words must be confirmed by the way you live your life. Your actions must acknowledge His presence, uniqueness, priority in your life, and His right to rule over you. Unfortunately this is a foreign concept to a lot of Christians, and it goes totally against what our culture is saying about life.

Be careful not to get the wrong idea about modeling the Christian life. God does not expect us to be perfect. But we should be growing and maturing in our relationship with Him. You can't cultivate a spiritually healthy home until you as a parent are attempting to live a life of obedience with Christ at the center of your own life.

A spiritually healthy home has a God-consciousness about it. There's a sense by each member that the Lord is present every minute and actively involved in what the family is doing. You foster this by praying, talking about God, and praising Him—more than just at mealtimes. Talk frequently about spiritual truths from the Bible and how they apply to everyday life. Discuss things like the beauty of creation, how Jesus wants to help those less fortunate, or even how the Bible relates to current events. Remember, your teens need to understand that having a relationship with Jesus involves more than just going to church on Sunday.

3. Help your teens develop a biblical world view.

With relative truth and values clarification permeating our culture, it's important for all of us to have a biblical world view. Researcher George Barna in his book *Think Like Jesus,* says a biblical world view incorporates critical Scriptural principles and translates those beliefs into specific action. You could say it is a kind of filter through which you see and live your life.

Moses instructed the parents of Israel: "And you must commit yourselves wholeheartedly to these commands that I am giving you today. Repeat them again and again to your children. Talk about them when you are at home and when you are away on a journey, when you are lying down and when you are getting up again" (Deuteronomy 6:6–7). God wants us to build biblical truth into everyday life and conversation. Teens need to know that God is interested and involved in every dimension of their lives, and that the Bible is totally relevant to life in the twenty-first century.

An easy place to start, when discussing a situation or life issue, is to ask them, "What would Jesus want us to do?" If they're not sure, encourage them to explore God's Word for answers. The best thing for you to do is to do this with them. As they search the Bible for direction, they are forming a solid biblical basis for their thoughts, words, and actions. Helping our teens fortify their minds with God's truth is essential for resisting the deceptive influences of witchcraft and the occult. We must be constantly aware of the spiritual battle mentioned in Ephesians 6:10–18.

4. Celebrate your teens' uniqueness.

Our culture is into competition and comparisons in a huge way. There's tremendous emphasis placed on appearance and performance. Our teens live in a world that often seems to have no absolutes. It's a world that rewards the prettiest, the strongest, the smartest, and the wealthiest. As our teens compete with a host of others for recognition, Satan loves to take advantage of their sense of inadequacy, disappointment, and failure by tempting them to find acceptance and fulfillment in the wrong places.

A spiritually healthy home is one where individual differences in appearance, ability, and performance are celebrated rather than being a source for divisiveness. Our teens must be accepted for who they are and encouraged to celebrate their own distinctive uniqueness as children of God. Basically, affirming and honoring our teens regularly can help to accomplish this. For example, set aside one mealtime each month in their honor. Prepare their favorite food, play some of their favorite music. During the meal have other family members describe how they appreciate the honored guest. You might want to take turns around the table completing this statement: "I think (this person) is special in our family because . . ." Try to keep these comments focused on character qualities rather than appearance or performance. If time permits, play their favorite game. Then do the same the next month for another child. After time, your kids may want to also include you in this process.

Unfortunately, most teens I talk with rarely have a meal with their mom or dad. When they do, it's usually interrupted by the TV or phone calls. I'd encourage you to make it a top priority to have at least three meals together as a family each week. You and your teen need time to connect. Turn off the TV at mealtimes; this will help provide a better atmosphere to have a conversation during the meal. And don't answer the phone—let voice mail pick it up. It will make a huge difference in your communication as a family when you eliminate these distractions.

Another way to celebrate the uniqueness of your teens is to show a genuine interest in their activities. When was the last time you attended a concert your teen was playing in or a sports event in which they were competing? We are all busy, but showing interest in their activities is huge to them. I remember attending a color guard competition that my daughter Kati was participating in. While I was waiting for her to return her equipment to the bus, I overheard one of her teammates on her cell phone talking with her brother. "But Mom and Dad promised they would be here tonight—what do you mean they went out to dinner instead? I hate them!" she said. Then she threw the cell phone out the window. Remember, they only live these moments once. Make it a priority to be involved in their lives.

Be careful not to only be involved in activities that you are partial to. For example, you may be into sports more than music. It will speak volumes if you learn to engage in activities that interest them—even if it's not as interesting to you.

Helping your teen to feel appreciated and special is crucial to building a spiritually healthy family.

5. Maintain an environment of love and forgiveness.

Everyone needs to know they are loved and accepted—especially teens. The love you convey to your children must be unconditional; it continually says, "I love you no matter what you do." The Bible puts it this way in 1 Peter 4:8, "Most important of all, continue to show deep love for each other, for love covers a multitude of sins." Your teens must know you love them whether they bring home an A or an F; whether they hit a home run or strike out; whether or not they make the cheerleading squad or the debate team.

For most teens, a significant way to express your love to them is the time you spend with them. You need to schedule quality and quantity time with them. Go for a walk, play a game, run an errand together, or grab a drink and sit down to talk together. It's not so much what you do or even how much money you spend to do it that's important. It's that you consistently reserve time to be together. Time together communicates love.

Forgiveness is a significant element of unconditional love. You may discipline your teen for something they've done, but in the process they need to know that you forgive them for their misbehavior or irresponsibility. Forgiveness is never easy for us, but it is something that must be obeyed biblically. "Make allowance for each other's faults and forgive the person who offends you. Remember, the Lord forgave you, so you must forgive others" (Colossians 3:13). Unforgiveness leads to bitterness, which is like cancer to our soul. Unforgiveness is one of Satan's most effective weapons in our lives.

It's important that we as parents not only model forgiveness but also teach our teens to ask God's forgiveness and to seek the forgiveness of any person they have wronged. We need to demonstrate by example, take responsibility for our actions, and help them to do the same. When my son Tony was a senior in high school, he was having fun with some friends one night and things got a little out of control. The kids he was with decided to egg a classmate's house in our neighborhood. Tony drove the vehicle while the other kids pelted the house with raw eggs—some of which made their way to the roof. Needless to say the neighbors were not happy—especially when they had to hire someone to power-clean the egg off their roof. Tony was the only one positively identified because of his car. Most of the other kids bailed when it came time to take responsibility for what happened, which included cleaning up the mess and paying for the roof to be cleaned. I was proud of Tony for owning up to his actions, apologizing, and doing his part in the clean-up process. He learned a valuable lesson about forgiveness and responsibility.

Remember, once you forgive your teen, don't bring up the offense again in a critical way.

Once again, the best way for your teen to learn how to confess his or her misdeeds and ask forgiveness is through your example. I have been humbled on more than one occasion when I've had to ask one of my children to forgive me after I've said or done something to hurt them. But it's so awesome when I hear one of them say to me, "Dad, I forgive you and I still love you." If you don't admit your faults and seek forgiveness from your children, you are not only opening yourself up for spiritual conflicts, you are teaching your kids to do the same.

6. Establish consistent family devotions.

A great tool in helping to insulate your teen against witchcraft is to diligently nurture them with God's Word and prayer. Colossians 3:16 instructs us: "Let the words of Christ, in all their richness, live in your hearts and make you wise. Use his words to teach and counsel each other. Sing psalms and hymns and spiritual songs to God with thankful hearts."

Family devotions should be brief and simple. Read one or two Bible verses and discuss their application. You may also want to try memorizing verses together. Conclude your time together with conversational, down-to-earth prayer about the concerns of the family as a whole and each individual member. It doesn't have to be long and drawn out. But be sensitive and don't force your teen to pray; it may take some time before they are comfortable with conversational prayer.

7. Make prayer a priority.

It's been said that Satan believes in prayer, not because he practices it, but because he suffers from it. We need to help our teens recognize the incredible resource for resisting that is available to them in prayer. They need to learn that God is interested in everything that touches their lives—every relationship, event, circumstance, and problem. As well as that, He hears and answers their prayers.

However, prayer will only become a significant part of your teen's life when they see it practiced by you. For example, how often do you pray together as a family apart from mealtimes? Do you consistently bring the needs of your family to God in prayer as an individual? As a family? Do you turn to the Lord first, or pray as a last resort? Do you pray consistently with and for your teen? The importance you give to prayer in your home will radically shape the importance your child gives to prayer.

There's nothing like answered prayer in the family to motivate you and your teen to pray. A simple way to maintain that encouragement and motivation is to keep a family prayer journal. When you and your teen pray about something, write down the date you prayed and the specific request. Then when God answers the prayer, record the date and thank God together for His goodness and faithfulness. Look back at the answers recorded in your journal for encouragement when other requests are not answered as quickly. This journal can serve as a tangible reminder to your teen that God hears and answers prayer.

Remember not only to pray with your teen but also to pray for them consistently and specifically.

A Final Thought

We've talked about a lot of things in this book—some of which may seem frightening and overwhelming to you. Don't get discouraged. Don't panic! Or as your son or daughter may say to you, "Chill out!" There's a Chinese proverb that says, "A journey of a thousand miles begins with a single step." This is great wisdom for parenting. Take it one day at a time. Ask God to give you patience, wisdom, and courage. It's going to be costly—especially in terms of time. But it will be worth everything you invest to protect your teen. Someday you and your teen will be able to look back and see how the Lord worked in the midst of a tumultuous time in your family's life.

Commit yourself to do whatever it takes to protect your teen from today's witchcraft, and you'll be glad you did.

APPENDIX A:

QUICK REFERENCE COMPARISON GUIDE

WICCA, WITCHCRAFT, AND CHRISTIANITY

- Most Wiccans believe in some form of reincarnation.[1] For witches, reincarnation is different from what a Buddhist or Hindu believes. Instead of an endless "karma," witches view reincarnation as something positive that takes the soul upward in its advancement toward godhood.[2] Christians do not believe there are additional chances to come back and keep advancing your soul to new levels. The Bible is very clear when it says we die only once and then we are judged (Hebrews 9:26–28; 2 Peter 2:9).

- Wiccans believe they can influence reality through invoking invisible spirits and powers. They believe that magick is the craft of witchcraft.[3] Using magick, witchcraft, or invisible spirits is detestable to God and something He will not tolerate (Deuteronomy 18:9–13; Isaiah 8:19).

---

[1]Starhawk, *The Spiral Dance: A Rebirth of the Ancient Religions of the Great Goddess* (San Francisco: Harper & Row, 1979), 84.
[2]Ceisiwr Serith, *The Pagan Family: Handing the Old Ways Down* (St. Paul: Llewellyn Publications, 1994), 198.
[3]Starhawk, 13, 109.

- The Wiccan view of salvation can be summed up with this statement: "We can open new eyes and see that there is nothing to be saved from; no struggle of life against the universe, no God outside the world to be feared and obeyed."[4] Christians believe that we are all born with a spiritual terminal disease called sin that causes us to disobey God and go our own willful way. This causes us to be separated from God. The remedy was Christ's death on the cross (Romans 3:23, 6:23; Isaiah 59:2; 1 Timothy 2:5; 1 Peter 3:18).

- Wiccans believe that experience is a more important revelation than any code of belief, and that it's more important to reveal your own truth than to rely on doctrine. Christians believe that the most important revelation of truth is the Bible (Psalm 119:47, 72, 97; 2 Timothy 3:16; Hebrews 4:12).

- Wiccans worship the earth and creation. They recognize the divinity of nature and all living things.[5] Christians believe in worshiping the Creator, not the creation (Deuteronomy 4:39; Romans 1:25; Jude 25).

- Wiccans believe that people have their own divine nature: "Thou art Goddess, thou art God."[6] Christians believe that even though we are created in God's image, humanity is still sinful and fallen (Genesis 1:26–27; Romans 5:12). The Bible clearly teaches that all kinds of wickedness come from within a person, not some type of divinity (Jeremiah 17:9; Mark 7:14–23).

- Wiccans do not believe that Jesus was God in the flesh or Creator of the universe. They view Jesus as "a great white witch who knew the Coven of Thirteen."[7] The key principle that sets Christianity apart from any other religion is the belief that Jesus is God. One of the names for Jesus in the Bible is Immanuel, which means "God with us" (Matthew 1:21–23; John 1:1, 14, 18; 8:24; Philippians 2:5–6).

---

[4]Ibid., 14.
[5]Prudence Jones and Caitlin Matthews, eds., *Voices From the Circle: The Heritage of Western Paganism* (Wellingborough, Northamptonshire, England: The Aquarian Press, 1990), 40.
[6]Margot Adler, *Drawing Down the Moon: Witches, Druids, Goddess-Worshippers, and Other Pagans in America Today* (Boston: Beacon Press, 1986), 9.
[7]Doreen Valienete, *An ABC of Witchcraft: Past and Present* (New York: St. Martin's Press, 1973), 14.

APPENDIX B:

THE WICCAN REDE AND THE THREEFOLD LAW

WICCAN REDE

Bide ye the Wiccan laws ye must,
in perfect love and perfect trust.
Ye must live and let live,
fairly take and fairly give.
Cast the Circle thrice about,
to keep unwelcome spirits out.
To bind the spell well every time,
let the spell be spoken in rhyme.
Soft of eye and light of touch,
speak ye little and listen much.
Deosil go by waxing moon,
chanting out the Wiccan runes.
Widdershins go by waning moon,
chanting out the baneful tune.
When the Lady's moon is new,
kiss the hand to Her times two.
When the moon rides at Her peak,
then the heart's desire seek.
Heed the North wind's mighty gale:
lock the door and trim the sail.

When the wind comes from the
    South,
love will kiss thee on the mouth.
When the Moor wind blows from
    the West,
departed spirits have no rest.
When the wind blows from the East,
expect the new and set the feast.
Nine woods in the cauldron go,
burn them quick and burn them
    slow.
Elder be the Lady's tree,
burn it not or cursed ye'll be.
When the wheel begins to turn,
let the Beltane fires burn.
When the wheel has turned to Yule,
light the log and the Horned One
    rules.
Heed ye flower, bush and tree,
by the Lady, Blessed Be.

Where the rippling waters go,
cast a stone, the truth to know.
When ye have and hold a need,
hearken not to others' greed.
With a fool no seasons spend,
or be counted as his friend.
Merry meet and merry part,
bright the cheeks and warm the
    heart.

Mind the Threefold Law ye should,
three times bad and three times
    good.
When misfortune is enow,
wear the blue star on thy brow.
True in love ye must be,
lest thy love be false to thee.
These words the Wiccan Rede fulfill:
An ye harm none, do what ye will.[1]

Translation: You can basically do anything in the world that you want to, so long as it doesn't cause harm to yourself or anyone else.

THE THREEFOLD LAW

"Ensure that your actions are honorable, for all that you do shall return to you, threefold, good or bane."

Translation: If you do something nasty, eventually something three times as nasty will happen to you. If you do something good, eventually something three times as good will happen to you.

---

[1] *The Rede of the Wiccae* (*The Rede*) is commonly attributed to Lady Gwen (Gwynne) Thompson, a Celtic Traditionalist who submitted the poem as it was given to her by her grandmother, Adriana Porter.

GLOSSARY OF WICCAN/ WITCHCRAFT TERMS

Affirmation. A positive, repetitive declaration about something you want to manifest in your life. It always needs to be in the positive and present form.

Akasha. A Sanskrit word used to describe the concept of Spirit. It's the fifth element—the omnipresent spiritual power that permeates the universe and unifies the other four elements (fire, water, earth, and air).

Akashic Records. Edgar Cayce, a noted psychic, developed the concept of a place on the astral plane where there's a huge collection of information on everyone who has ever lived and ever will live. Facts about people like who they were, what they accomplished, when they were born, and when they will die are found here.

Altar. A working surface, like a tabletop, that's to be used only for magickal or religious purposes. It can be round, square, triangular, oblong, or oval.

Amulet. An object that has been magickally empowered to protect one from a specific type of negative energy.

Animism. The concept that the entire earth is a living organism is a widespread belief in neopagan religions. The word *animism* means "soul" or "breath." Some witches even view animism as "the heart and soul" of ancient witchcraft. Some Wiccans even believe that matter like rocks are alive and that all objects in the universe have some kind of inner consciousness.

Archetype. Represents a character or set of human characteristics to all people throughout all cultures. It can also mean "original model," like the characters of a myth.

Astral Travel. The ability for the spirit to leave the body and visit other places and times.

Athame. A Wiccan ritual knife. It usually has a double-edged blade with a black handle. Most of the time it is used to direct personal power during ritual workings.

Augury. The art, ability, or practice of divination by signs and omens.

Aura. "Invisible breath." Witches see aura as a kind of energy atmosphere that surrounds each living thing.

Balefire. A bonfire or a smaller fire that is lit for magickal purposes.

Banishing Magick. Using your will to make something go away.

Beltane. A Wiccan Sabbat celebrated on April 30 or May 1. Beltane is also known as May Eve, Roodmas, Walpurgis Night, or Cethsamhain. Beltane celebrates the symbolic union of the goddess and god.

Besom. Broom.

Bind. To bind a spell is to complete its casting, releasing it to do its work independently of the weaver of the spell.

Binding. A binding spell ties up or restrains a person's negative behavior but not the person.

Blessing Way. An alternative to the conventional baby shower. This ritual offers nurture and support for the mother-to-be, prayers for the ease and safety of the birth, and prayers for the baby's health and good life.

Book of Shadows. A collection of spiritual lessons, spells, magickal rules, and other information that is written down in a journal as a reference book. No one true Book of Shadows exists; they are all relevant to their respective users. Each one is a personal record of the individual's progress and work.

Book of the Dead. An Egyptian treatise on the afterlife that includes hundreds of magickal instructions for everything from invocations to charms.

Caduceus. A wand or staff with two snakes twined around it. At the top of the wand is a pair of wings.

Cakes and Ale. The Wiccan communion that consists of a natural beverage and cake offered to each participant in a ritual.

Cauldron. Any three-legged pot, which many witches and Wiccans use to represent the threefold goddess.

Censer. A heat-proof container in which incense is burned. It symbolizes the element of air.

Ceremony of Initiation. A ceremony of honor conducted by a group welcoming an initiate into the craft.

Chakra. Means "wheel" in Sanskrit. They are round, spinning discs of energy that lie along the spine from the tailbone to the top of the head. Taoists, Hindus, Hopis, and Tibetans all use chakra systems to explain different energies in the body.

Chalice. A drinking vessel, generally handleless and comprising a bowl, stem, and base, used in Wicca to represent the element of water.

Chant. A series of meaningful words that the witch repeats to focus his or her will and raise energy toward a specific goal.

Charge. To infuse an object with personal power. An act of magick.

Charm. An object that a person associates with luck or another form of protection.

Cingulam. A knotted cord worn with ritual robes; it often denotes connection to a coven or degreed status.

Circle. A space marked out and consecrated by a witch or witches for the purposes of protection or a ritual.

Clairvoyance. Literally means "clear-seeing" and describes the ability of an individual to sense messages or visions using means other than the five human senses.

Conscious Mind. That part of our minds at work while we perform acts related to the physical world.

Cone of Power. A combination of love, creativity, and spirit that forms the basis of a witch's power. He or she then uses this energy to accomplish a desire.

Coven. A group of witches, usually centered on one or two leaders, who practice their religion together. The word most likely comes from the Middle English word *covent*, which means "a gathering."

Craft. Wicca, witchcraft, folk magick. Among other things, it is the art of using witchcraft power to influence future events. The word comes from "witch" (a wise one) and "craft" (strength and skill).

Crone. The third and eldest aspect of the goddess.

Crucible. A container made to heat metal at a high temperature. Also defined as a test or a trial.

Crystal. A stone with a particular, regular molecular structure. For magickal purposes it's not necessary to make a distinction between crystals and other minerals.

Curse. An appeal to supernatural powers for injury or harm to another.

Dark Ages. An era from about A.D. 476 to about the year 1000 characterized by repression and un-enlightenment.

Dedication. An individual's statement, through ceremony, that affirms his or her dedication to craft laws, structure, and to deity.

De-magicking. The process of returning magickal energies back to the earth.

Deosil. A clockwise motion, or the direction in which the shadow on a sundial moves as the sun "moves" across the sky. In the Wiccan dance, deosil is thought to generate energy with positive qualities.

Devas. A natural order of spirits (like fairies) with elemental essence.

Diabolism. The invocation of devils.

Divination. The magickal art of discovering the unknown by interpreting random patterns or symbols. Tools such as clouds, tarot cards, flames, or smoke are used. Divination contacts the psychic mind by tricking or drowsing the conscious mind through ritual and by observing or manipulating tools.

Druid. A priest or priestess of Celtic Europe who carried out social and religious functions.

Eclectic Witchcraft. An individual approach in which a witch picks and chooses from many different traditions and creates a personalized form of witchcraft that meets his or her needs and abilities.

Elements. Earth, air, fire, water. These four essences are the building blocks of the universe. Everything that exists or has the potential to exist contains one or more of these energies.

Elementals. The beings that live within the energy force of a specific element.

Elixir. A kind of potion used to energize, improve, and restore overall health to the person drinking it.

Ephemeris. A book that shows where the planets are every day of the year. Before computers, astrologers would use this and a lot of brain power to calculate charts.

Equinox. Means "equal night." Twice a year, the duration of daylight and night are equal. This is a traditional time for many Wiccan celebrations, marking two of the major points on the Wheel of the Year.

Esbat. A Wiccan ritual usually occurring on the full moon and dedicated to the goddess in her lunar aspect.

ESP. Extrasensory perception encompasses most paranormal abilities such as telepathy and clairvoyance.

Evocation. Calling up spirits or other nonphysical entities to either visible appearance or invisible attendance. This is not necessarily a Wiccan practice. Compare with *invocation.*

Evoke. What witches do when they project energy from within themselves out into the universe.

Eye of Newt. The newt is related to the salamander. The incorporation of the eye refers to vision. The term means "to receive supernatural foresight."

Fairy Dust. A super-fine glitter, similar to embossing powder. Some people buy it in vials, keep the vials closed, and wear them as magickal jewelry.

Familiar. An animal that acts in the capacity of a magickal partner, guide, and teacher to a witch.

Fetish. An object believed to have a specific magickal power for which that object is then carried, buried, burned, or otherwise utilized magickally.

Fire Festivals. First consisting of Beltane and Samhain, Imbolc and Lammas were added at a later date. These four festivals are associated with planting, harvesting, and hunting ceremonies.

Folk Magic. The magic of the people. The practice of projecting personal power, as well as the energies within natural objects such as herbs and crystals, to bring about needed change.

Goddess Mother. A Wiccan godmother.

Great Rite. A celebration of the god and goddess in literal or figurative terms so that the two can be united to create balance and increased power for magick.

Green Man. An image of the god aspect of divinity that is strongly connected with nature.

Group Mind. The establishing of perfect love and perfect trust among a group of individuals.

Handfasting. A Wiccan marriage ceremony. A couple (man and woman, two men, two women) is joined together for as long as their love shall last. If they decide they no longer love each other, they can split.

Hex/hexing. Derived from a German word for *witch,* describing the casting of a spell. Used synonymously with curse.

Higher Self. A spiritual part of humankind that has access to the universal mind and all the knowledge and wisdom of our past lives.

High Priest and Priestess. Individuals who have advanced knowledge of witchcraft and lead a coven.

Image Candle. A candle infused with a witch's unmatched energy, personality, and power.

Incantation. A chant with the intention of bringing magick into one's life.

Imbolc. A Wiccan Sabbat celebrated on February 2, also known as Candlemas, Lupercalia, Feast of Pan, Feast of Torches, Feast of Waxing Light, Oimelc, and Brigit's Day. Imbolc celebrates the first stirrings of spring and the recovery of the goddess from giving birth to the sun (the god) at Yule.

Immanent. Something that exists or remains within. It can be something inherent.

Initiation. A process whereby an individual is introduced or admitted into a group, interest, skill, or religion. A candidate of Wicca often undergoes it. Initiations can be ritual occasions and can also occur spontaneously.

Invocation. An appeal or petition to a higher power (or powers) such as the god or goddess (lord and the lady). A prayer. Invocation is actually a method of establishing conscious ties with those aspects of the goddess and god that dwell within us. In essence, then, we seemingly cause them to appear or make themselves known by becoming aware of them.

Kabbalah. The occult theosophy with rabbinical origins. It's an obscure interpretation of Hebrew scriptures with strong ritualistic overtones.

Karma. The law of karma is simply cause and effect. For every action, there is an equal reaction. It demonstrates that whatever you do will come back to you.

Kemetic Witchcraft. An attempt to exactly re-create ancient Egyptian witchcraft, usually one particular time period in ancient Egyptian history.

Labrys. A double-edged axe that symbolized the goddess in ancient Crete and still used by some Wiccans for the same purpose. The two axe heads represent the goddess in her lunar aspect.

Law of Attraction. What you put out is what will come to you.

Left-Hand Path. Black magick, which is used to manipulate free will or cause harm.

Libations. In Wicca, an offering to the goddess and god of wine (or another beverage) blessed within the circle. Can also be used in Wicca to include the offering of whatever food was shared during the circle as well.

Lughnassah. A Wiccan Sabbat celebrated on August 1. Also known as August Eve, Lammas, and Feast of Bread. Lughnasadh marks the first harvest, when the fruits of the earth are cut and stored for the dark winter months and the god mysteriously weakens as the days grow shorter.

Mabon. A Wiccan Sabbat occurring on or around September 21, the Autumnal Equinox. Mabon is a celebration of the second harvest, when nature prepares for winter. Mabon is a remnant of ancient harvest festivals.

Maiden. Coven's right-hand woman. A skilled individual who assists the high priest and high priestess.

Magic. Comes from the root meaning "to be able, to have power." Magic is what an entertainer does on stage—card tricks, making things disappear, sawing someone in half, etc.

Magick. Comes from the same root as *magic* but is in the realm of witches and may include spells, healing, the harnessing of psychic forces, and divination. It is the direction and application of energy. Spelled with a *k* to distinguish the belief in using the universe's energy for spiritual purposes from the magical illusions performed by entertainers.

Magick Circle. A two-dimensional circle constructed of personal power in which Wiccan rituals are usually enacted. It is created through visualization and magick. The circle completely surrounds and protects you.

Magickal Correspondence. Items, objects, days, colors, moon phases, oils, angels, and herbs used in rituals that match the intent of the celebration or ceremony.

Magick Witchcraft Temple. A special room (or outdoor location) where witches perform their magic. It is also a storage place for candles, textbooks, and other equipment. On the floor are painted two concentric magick circles.

Magnus. A magician or sorcerer.

Manifesting Magick. Using one's will to make something happen.

Meditation. Reflection, contemplation—turning inward toward self, or outward toward deity or nature. A quiet time in which the practitioner may either dwell upon particular thoughts or symbols or allow them to come unbidden.

Medium. A person who has the ability to become a middle ground between our world and the world of the dead, therefore allowing the dead to speak through him or her.

Metaphysical. Events that occur beyond physical explanations.

Midsummer. The summer solstice, and Wiccan festival, occurring on or near June 21. Midsummer marks the time of the year when the sun (the god) is symbolically at the height of his powers.

Mirror Book. A witch's personal account of his or her growth and evolution as a witch.

Neopagan. "New Pagan." A member or follower of one of the newly formed pagan religions now spreading throughout the world. All Wiccans are pagans, but not all pagans are Wiccans.

Neopaganism. It basically means a system of worshiping nature and the gods of nature.

Numerology. The metaphysical science of numbers. It is supposed to help people discover who they are, where they're going, and who they will become.

Occult. A set of mostly unrelated divination and/or spiritual practices or activities which appear to tap into forces that have not been explained by science, and which are not conventional practices seen in traditional religions.

Occultism. The belief in practices like alchemy, astrology, divination, and magick that are all based on "hidden knowledge" about the universe and its mystifying forces. People who practice the occult try to tap into this invisible knowledge to bring about whatever effects they wish for.

Old Ones. A Wiccan term sometimes used to encompass all aspects of the goddess and god.

Oracle. A person of great knowledge who speaks the wisdom of spirit.

Ordains. A set of practical, spiritual, and coven laws that govern those involved in Wicca.

Ostara. Occurs around March 21 at the spring equinox. Ostara marks the beginning of true, astronomical spring, when snow and ice make way for green. As such, Ostara is a fire and fertility Sabbat, celebrating the return of the sun, the god, and the fertility of the earth (the goddess).

Otherworld. The world where spirits abide, waiting to be reborn.

Ouija. A board that has the letters, numbers, and other signs written on it and that is used together with a planchette to seek messages of spiritualistic or telepathic origin.

Pagan. Derived from the Latin *paganus*, meaning *peasant* or *hut dweller*. Pagan religions are natural religions both in origin and in mode of expression as opposed to artificially created ideological religions. Pagan is also a general term for magick embracing religions, such as Wicca, Druid, and Shaman. Sometimes used interchangeably with NeoPagan.

Paganism. In general, this term is accepted as an umbrella term for Wiccans, Shamans, Druids, the craft, and an assortment of others whose beliefs are polytheistic, nature-oriented, and in some way focus on magick.

Palmistry. The art of reading the hands. From a person's hands you can supposedly learn a lot about them physically, mentally, and emotionally. Apparently a hand will also tell you about a person's past, present, and future.

Pantheon. The collection of all the deities from one culture. It can also be a temple that has been dedicated to all of the gods.

Pentacle. A ritual object (usually a circular piece of wood, metal, clay, etc.) upon which a five-pointed star (pentagram) is inscribed, painted, or engraved, point up, with a circle around the star. It represents the earth, air, fire, water, and spirit of the human, encompassed by the never-ending love (circle) of spirit. The words *pentacle* and *pentagram* are not interchangeable.

Pentagram. The basic interlaced five-pointed star, visualized with one point upward. The pentagram represents the five senses, elements (earth, air, fire, water, and akasha), the hand, and the human body. It is a symbol of power and is a protective symbol known to have been in use since the days of old Babylon. Today it is frequently associated with Wicca.

Personal Altar. A surface designated by a witch to represent his or her place of power.

Personal Power. That energy which sustains our bodies. It originates within the goddess and god. We first absorb it from our biological mother within the womb, and later from food, water, the moon and sun, and other natural objects. We release it during movement, exercise, sex, conception, and childbirth. Magick is a movement of personal power for a specific goal.

Planetary Hours. A system of hourly division associated with planetary energies.

Poppet. A magickal doll. A witch concentrates on the magick he or she wants to do while making a poppet. Related to the word *puppet*.

Potion. A liquid contrived with magickal components and through magickal processes to produce a specific result.

Power. The subtle energy that comes from the mind. In Germany it is called "vril" and in India "prana." Those who practice martial arts call it "chi."

Power/lineage. Energy and history passed from one person to another.

Psychic Mind. The subconscious or unconscious mind, in which people receive psychic impressions. The psychic mind is at work when people sleep, dream, and meditate. It is the direct link with the divine, and with the larger, non-physical world around us.

Psychism. The act of being consciously psychic, in which the psychic mind and conscious mind are linked and working in harmony. Also known as psychic awareness.

Rede. An archaic word that means "advice" or "counsel." In Wicca it is a good rule to live by. Also see *Wiccan Rede*.

Reincarnation. The belief that life and death are a cycle. After leaving this life, the soul spends time in the spirit world until it is reborn to experience various situations and perspectives. One of the doctrines of Wicca.

Ritual. Ceremony. A specific form of movement. A manipulation of objects or inner processes designed to produce desired effects. In religion, ritual is geared toward union with the divine. In magick it produces a specific state of consciousness that allows the magician to move energy toward needed goals. A spell is a magick ritual.

Ritual Consciousness. A specific, alternate state of awareness necessary to the successful practice of magick. The magician achieves this consciousness through the use of visualization and ritual. It is an attunement of the conscious mind with the psychic mind, a state in which the magician senses energies, gives them purpose, and releases them toward the magick goal. It is heightening of the senses, an expanded awareness of the nonphysical world, a linking with nature and with the forces behind all conceptions of deity.

Ritual Purification. The practice of cleansing the body and mind prior to performing a ritual.

Runes. They are basically old alphabets that were used by the ancient Germans, Scandinavians, and Anglo-Saxons. Each letter in the runic alphabet also has magickal and symbolic meaning. These symbols are once again widely being used in magick and divination.

Sabbat. A Wiccan holiday.

Sacred Space. Witches will often create a "sacred space" where they can work their magick. This entails putting up a protective sphere of energy (often called a magick circle). The magick circle holds energy in place and keeps negative influences outside. When the work is finished, the sacred space is dismissed.

Samhain. A Wiccan Sabbat celebrated on October 31, also known as November Eve, Hallowmass, Halloween, Feast of Souls, Feast of the Dead, Feast of Apples. Samhain marks the symbolic death of the sun god and his passing into the "land of the young," where he awaits rebirth of the Mother Goddess at Yule. This Celtic word is pronounced by Wiccans as "SOW-wen" (the "sow" sounds like the first three letters in sour).

Sanskrit. The ancient language of India.

Scry. To gaze at or into an object (a quartz crystal sphere, pool of water, reflections, a candle flame) to still the conscious mind in order to contact the psychic mind. This practice allows the scryer to become aware of events prior to their actual occurrence, as well as to perceive past or present events through ways other than the five senses. A form of divination.

Shaman. A medicine man or priest from a non-technological culture. Shamans engage in a lot of different activities, including astral projection, fasting, sleep deprivation, and drugs to help themselves attain altered states of consciousness.

Shrine. A sacred place that holds a collection of objects representing deity.

Sigil. A magickal sign, seal, or image. Used for everything from inscribing magick tools to letter writing to empowering a poppet.

Simple Feast. A ritual meal shared with the goddess and god.

Skyclad. Literally means "clothed by the sky" (naked), used to describe ritualistic worship without clothing.

Smudging. A ritual used whenever or wherever the need is felt to cleanse, balance, protect, or purify oneself, others, a room, one's crystals, or other specific tools. Smoke from an embering bundle of sage is used.

Solitary Witch. A witch who practices and works alone.

Spell. A magickal recipe used to affect change. It has a number of components including chanting, ritual, meditation, visualization, and magickal objects.

Spirits of the Stones. The elemental energies naturally inherent within the four directions of the earth. They are personified within the standing stones tradition as the "Spirits of the Stones," and in other Wiccan traditions as the "Lords of the Watchtowers." They are linked with the elements.

Spirit. The overall energy that runs the universe in a harmonious way. Also referred to as the lord and lady—the feminine and masculine side of God.

Sorcery. The use of magick accessible to ordinary people; such as setting out offerings to helpful spirits or using charms.

Summerland. Wiccan version of heaven. Where spirits go after death to rest and reflect in the company of the god and goddess, and to decide how they are going to reincarnate.

Sympathy. A universal law that associates objects with like objects.

Talisman. An object charged with personal power to attract a specific force or energy to its bearer.

Tameran Witchcraft. Any modern form of witchcraft based at least in part on ancient Egyptian witchcraft, including some forms of eclectic witchcraft and some forms of Wicca.

Taoism. A Chinese religion/philosophy with several similarities to the craft—especially the emphasis on spiritual polarity. In Taoism this is conceived by the yin and yang; in Wicca it's the goddess and god, as well as the interconnectedness of all things.

Tarot Cards. A divination tool that people have used for centuries.

Tarot Spread. The pattern in which the cards are laid out when doing a reading. There are a lot of different spreads that can be used.

Telekinesis. The moving of a stationary object—without touching it—by using the power of the mind. It's a direct influence of mind over matter, causing movement without demonstrating physical energy or force.

Temple Summoner. Coven's right-hand man. A skilled individual who assists the High Priest and High Priestess.

Theban Script. A form of writing that helps focus a witch's energy and send it into the object that you are inscribing.

Third Eye. One of the chakras, positioned in the center of the forehead and associated with the pineal gland. The chakra is related to the power of inner vision, both active visualization and the ability to see between the worlds.

Totem. An animal symbol or spirit that guides one throughout life.

Tradition, Wiccan. An organized, structured, specific Wiccan subgroup, which is usually initiatory, often with unique ritual practices. Many traditions have their own Books of Shadows, and usually recognize members of other traditions as Wiccan. Most traditions are composed of a number of covens as well as solitary practitioners.

Underworld. The opposite of the living. According to mythology, it was formally earth but then came under the rule of Hades, the Greek god of the dead.

Visualization. The process of forming mental images. Magickal visualization consists of forming images of needed goals during ritual. Visualization is also used to direct personal power and natural energies for various purposes during magick, including charging and forming the magick circle. It is a function of the conscious mind. The practice of training your mind to "see" an object in your thoughts to bring it to you on the physical plane.

Voodoo. A charm that is thought to embody magickal powers or to bewitch by, or as if by, a voodoo. It is also a religious cult practiced mainly in Caribbean countries—especially Haiti—and involves animistic deities.

Wand. A tool made of wood or metal used to cast or direct energy.

Wards. Mystical energy patterns designed to safeguard a person or area from negative influences. They are often drawn in the air at the four quarters of a sacred space to enforce the protective energy.

Warlock. Another word for traitor. It is not used to describe a male witch. A male witch is also called a witch or a Wiccan.

Watchtowers. Sometimes referred to as the "Guardians of the Watchtowers," they are powerful entities associated with the four elements and the four directions. They are said to be very powerful, and some witches view them as archangels.

White-Handled Knife. A normal cutting knife with a sharp blade and a white handle. It is used within Wicca to cut herbs and fruits, to slice bread during the simple feast, and for other functions but never for sacrifice. Sometimes called the "bolline."

White Witchcraft. "Positive" witchcraft, associated with goodness, not evil.

Wicca. From the Anglo-Saxon word *wicce*, which means to shape or bend nature to one's service. A loosely connected group of about 150 modern Western witchcraft religions. It is also known as the practice of folk magick (the magick of the people). It is a contemporary pagan religion with spiritual roots in the earliest expressions of reverence of nature. Some of its major identifying motifs are: reverence for the goddess and god, acceptance of reincarnation and magic, ritual observance of astronomical and agricultural phenomena, and the creation and use of spheroid temples for ritual purposes.

Wiccan Rede. The ethic by which Wiccans live. The Rede can be summarized by the following eight-word statement: "An ye harm none, do what ye will." It is the code by which all Wiccans must adhere.

Widdershins. A counterclockwise motion in the Wiccan dance that is thought to draw energy with negative qualities. It is usually used in the Northern Hemisphere for negative magical purposes, or for dispersing negative energies or conditions such as disease. Southern Hemisphere Wiccans may use widdershins motions for exactly the opposite purposes; namely, for positive ends. In either case, widdershins and deosil motions are symbolic; only strict, closed-minded traditionalists believe that accidentally walking around the altar backward, for instance, will raise negativity. Widdershins motions are still shunned by the majority of Wiccans, though some use it while, for instance, dispersing the magick circle at the end of a rite.

Witch. Someone who seeks to control the forces within him- or herself—that make life possible in order to live wisely and well without harm to others and in harmony with nature. In ancient times, a practitioner of the remnants of pre-Christian folk magick, particularly that kind related to herbs, stones, wells, and rivers. One who practices witchcraft.

Witchcraft. The craft of the witch—magick or sorcery—especially magick utilizing personal power in conjunction with the energies within stones, herbs, colors, and other natural objects. However, some followers of Wicca use this word to denote their religion. The term is used in many different ways in different places and times.

Witches' Pyramid. A creed and structure of learning that witches follow. It can be summarized as: to know, to dare, to will, and to be silent.

Wortcunning. The art of growing and using herbs for magickal and healing purposes.

Wyrt. The Old English word for "plant" or "herb."

Yin and Yang. They are archetypal opposites—the negative, passive, and female versus the positive, active, and male. From Chinese Taoist philosophy.

Yule. A Wiccan Sabbat celebrated on or about December 21, marking the rebirth of the sun god from the earth goddess. Yule occurs at the winter solstice.

Note: Most of these definitions come from Wiccan and witchcraft literature/ sources.

APPENDIX D:

WICCAN HOLIDAYS AND THE WHEEL OF THE YEAR

Greater Sabbats

- Samhain (Halloween): October 31
- Beltane (Rudemas): April 30th/May 1
- Imbolc (Candlemas): February 2
- Lughnassah (Lammas): July 30/August 1

Lesser Sabbats

- Winter Solstice (Yule): December 21/22
- Spring Equinox (Ostara): March 21/22
- Summer Solstice (Midsummer Eve): June 21/22
- Autumn Equinox (Mabon): September 21/22

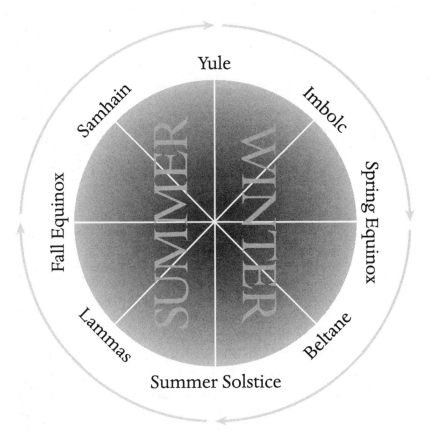

WHEEL OF THE YEAR

APPENDIX E:

SYMBOLS

Pentagram. A five-pointed star, with the sides interwoven. It has also been called the Endless Knot because it can be drawn with a single line. Generally, the top point represents the spirit (Akasha) and the other points represent wind, fire, earth, and water—substances that are crucial to all life. It has become the symbol of witchcraft, Wicca, and neopaganism. Some witches also view the five points as representing the three aspects of the goddess—maiden, mother, and crone, and the two aspects of the god—dark and light.

Pentacle. A pentagram with a circle drawn around it.

Sacred Spirals. Represents the dance of divine energy within the world of a witch. Drawn clockwise, the sacred spiral brings things inward; drawn counterclockwise, the spiral pushes negative energies away. The spiral also signifies the ancient journey within.

Equal-Armed Cross. Represents another powerful magickal symbol. This cross stands for many ideals—the four seasons, the four directions, the four archangels, the four winds, and the four quarters of the magick circle. Drawn in the air or on paper from top to bottom and right to left with the right hand, the symbol represents healing energies. Drawn from top to bottom and left to right with the left hand signifies banishing negative energies. A witch also employs the equal-armed cross to "seal" a magickal working so that negative energies cannot reverse the positive efforts of the magickal person.

 ***Goddess symbol.*** The symbol of the goddess (full moon in the middle flanked by crescent moons) signifies the feminine aspect of spirit, women's mysteries, and the healing of the divine. Witches use this symbol to connect with the divine feminine and wear the image to show their faith in the Lady.

APPENDIX F:

CONTACT INFORMATION

For more information on how to purchase audio and video resources, CDs, drum stuff, and other books by Steve Russo, as well as information on the *Real Answers* and *Life on the Edge—Live!* radio programs, the *Real Answers* TV show, citywide evangelistic events, or public school assemblies, please contact:

Real Answers with Steve Russo
P.O. Box 1549
Ontario, CA 91762
(909) 466–7060
FAX (909) 466–7056
E-mail: Russoteam@realanswers.com

You can also visit our Web sites at:

www.realanswers.com
or
www.steverusso.com

Equipping Teens
for the Battle

Teens are bombarded daily with messages that blur the lines between Christianity and modern-day witchcraft. In his book written especially for teens, Steve Russo explains the dangers of Wicca and exposes the deception in the promises made by its followers. Russo demonstrates that the Christian faith is the only true way to fill needs in the lives of teenagers and gives practical tools to help teens deal with the growing popularity of Wicca.

What's the Deal With Wicca?
  by Steve Russo

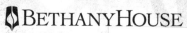

⬧BETHANYHOUSE